YOANI SÁNCHEZ, a University of Havana graduate in philology, emigrated to Switzerland in 2002. Two years later, she decided to return to Cuba, but promised herself she would live there as a free person and started her blog, *Generation Y*, upon her return. In 2008, *Time* Magazine named her one of the 100 Most Influential People in the World; it named *Generation Y* one of the "Best Blogs" of 2009. Spain honored her with its highest award for digital journalism, the Ortega y Gasset Prize. She has also been named one of the "100 Most Notable Hispanic Americans" by *El Pais* (Spain). In 2010 she received the World Press Freedom Hero award from the International Press Institute, and was named a "Young Global Leader" by the World Economic Forum.

In 2009 she became the first—and so far only—blogger to interview President Barack Obama, who commented that her blog "provides the world a unique window into the realities of daily life in Cuba," and applauded her efforts to "empower fellow Cubans to express themselves through the use of technology."

She lives with her husband, independent journalist Reinaldo Escobar and their son Teo in a high-rise apartment in Havana, overlooking Revolution Square.

Her blog is online in English at desdecuba.com/generationy

Translator **M.J. PORTER** lives in Seattle, where she is a partner in a transportation-consulting firm. She co-founded a cooperative translation site, HemosOido.com, where volunteers now translate the work of more than thirty Cuban bloggers into English, German, French, Italian, and Portuguese.

HAVANA REAL

HAVANA REAL

ONE WOMAN FIGHTS TO TELL THE TRUTH ABOUT CUBA TODAY

YOANI SÁNCHEZ

TRANSLATED BY M. J. PORTER

MELVILLEHOUSE
BROOKLYN, NEW YORK

Havana Real
Originally published in Italian, in an earlier form,
as *Cuba Libre: Vivere E Scrivere All'avana*
© 2009 RCS Libri SpA - Milano
Translation from Spanish © 2011 M.J. Porter
"Fidel Castro, present and past," originally published
in the *Washington Post*, August 5, 2010
First Melville House printing: March 2011

Melville House Publishing
145 Plymouth Street
Brooklyn, NY 11201

www.mhpbooks.com

ISBN: 978-1-935554-25-7

Printed in the United States of America

2 3 4 5 6 7 8 9 10

Library of Congress Cataloging-in-Publication Data

Sánchez, Yoani, 1975-
[Cuba libre. English]
Havana real : one woman fights to tell the truth about Cuba today /
Yoani Sanchez ; [translated by] M.J. Porter.
    p. cm.
ISBN 978-1-935554-25-7 (pbk.)
1. Sánchez, Yoani, 1975---Blogs. 2. Cuba--Social conditions--21st cen-
tury. 3. Cuba--History--1990- 4. Women journalists--Cuba--Biogra-
phy. I. Title.
F1760.S2813 2011
972.9107--dc22

                    2011005142

CONTENTS

INTRODUCTION

In 2004, Yoani Sánchez returned to Cuba two years after emigrating to Switzerland, where she and her family had planned to start a new life in a free and democratic country. Explaining a condition of her return, she said:

> I promised myself that I would live in Cuba as a free person, and accept the consequences.

This book is one of those consequences.

Yoani was born in 1975 in a tenement in Central Havana to parents who were just a few years older than the Revolution. She inherited her love of books from her father (an engineer on the national railway), worked hard at school, and proudly put the Little Pioneer scarf around her neck, vowing to "Be like Che!"

She was fourteen when the Berlin Wall fell and the Soviet Union cut most of its $6 billion annual subsidy to Cuba. Fidel Castro warned the nation that it was facing "a special period in a time of peace." Yoani's adolescence was marked by this Special Period, a time of terrible scarcity—when a word, *alumbrón*, was coined for the unusual situation of electricity being on; when fried grapefruit rinds took the place of meat in the national diet; when, it was rumored, melted condoms sometimes stood in for the cheese on a concoction that was anything but "pizza."

Yoani finished high school during the Special Period and was accepted to the University of Havana. She had dreams of becoming a journalist but instead found herself channeled into philology—the study of words. At 17, she met her future husband, Reinaldo Escobar, a fired-journalist-turned-elevator-mechanic, and when she was 19 their son, Teo, was born.

Though she continued to study after Teo's birth and went on to receive her degree, she did not pursue a career in academia. Her incendiary thesis, *Words Under Pressure: A Study of the Literature of the Dictatorship in Latin America*, assured that her scholarly interests would not be welcomed. She has no regrets.

Working as a freelance Spanish teacher and as a guide for German tourists allowed Yoani to help support her family, but it couldn't compensate for the disenchantment and economic suffocation of daily life under the Castro dictatorship. When she left for Switzerland in 2002, she was traveling a well-worn path, one taken by tens of thousands of Cubans every year. Her decision to return was far less common.

Before leaving for Switzerland, Yoani had already built her first computer out of spare parts. When she returned home, she, Reinaldo, and a few friends started the online magazine *Consensus*, with Yoani in the role of designer and webmaster.

In April 2007, combining her love of language with computing skills that she had further honed in Switzerland, she launched her own blog, *Generación Y*—the "Y" referring to the popularity of that letter in her generation's first names.

To post her entries she had to dress as a tourist and pretend to speak only German so she could sneak into hotel Internet cafés, at a time when burly bouncers enforced the law barring Cubans from tourist hotels.

The blog was a work in progress, and it wasn't until December of 2007 that she was able, for the first time, to provide her readers with the chance to comment. As she described it:

> In the moment of that first reader comment, I felt my blog come alive. Become its own being. Wherever I am, whatever I'm doing, even as I sleep, people are visiting Generation Y, talking to me, to each other, telling their own stories...yes, that's exactly what it's like... no, no it's not, you're crazy... stop, wait a minute... no, no, listen ... listen ... oye....

The reach and power of Yoani's blog soon grew. In early 2008, she was awarded Spain's most prestigious journalism prize, and *Time* magazine named her one of the "100 Most Influential People in the World." A few weeks later, the Cuban regime's "cyber response brigade" was finally able to block access to her blog throughout Cuba, and suddenly Yoani herself could no longer see her site. A team of helpers—led by a Cuban exile in Canada who had studied journalism with Reinaldo at the University of Havana—picked up the reins. From that point on, Yoani had to rely on the help of friends and strangers, e-mailing her entries for others to post.

When Gorki Aguila, the leader of the punk rock band Porno Para Ricardo, was arrested on a Monday in August of

2008 and charged with "pre-criminal dangerousness," Yoani and friends—in Cuba and abroad—drew on the growing influence of her blog and the power of the Internet. By Wednesday, the scheduled day for Aguila's trial, his plight was already in headlines around the world. The regime delayed the trial to let it all blow over, but on Friday, the international news media gathered outside the courtroom with their cameras and commentators. Later that evening Aguila walked free, with an almost certain four-year prison sentence reduced to a $25 fine.

For the first time, Cuba-watchers said, the power of the Internet launched from within the country had "pushed the wall." And Yoani's reach continued to expand. In 2009, she became the first (and, to date, the only) blogger to interview President Barack Obama.

Although she once called herself an "accidental blogger," Yoani was energized by the power of words floating in a cyberspace she could barely see. She and Reinaldo began a program to similarly energize others throughout Cuba, holding blogger-training sessions in other towns. In 2010, with the help of friends and fellow bloggers, they founded the Blogger Academy, which operates out of their living room. These efforts paid off as the number of Cuban bloggers exploded.

I first became aware of Yoani and *Generation Y* in late 2007, soon after a Canadian friend invited me to join her on a trip to Havana. It is not, in fact, illegal for Americans to go to Cuba—we just can't spend any money there. When my friend offered to make that problem go away, I couldn't board the plane fast enough. Anticipatory Internet surfing turned up Yoani's blog, and I was instantly captivated.

Soon I was flying into a warm winter island that was both oddly familiar and completely unexpected. Cuba looks exactly like its photos, and yet it feels *different*. I found that my Spanish—a grand total of five weeks of immersion classes—allowed me to have long and engaging conversations, and I fell in love with Cuba and Cubans. Something felt like home. Completely unforeseen, however, was the weight of the totalitarian state. Slowly, I began to feel that the intangible difference—the part that I couldn't quite get a handle on—was that weight.

Before I went to Cuba, I had read *Generation Y* in English translation, but soon after my return, the translations stopped appearing. I was struggling to read it in Spanish when Yoani posted a note saying she needed a new translator. I waited, but nothing happened. "Well," I thought, "someone has to do it." After struggling for three days over the first three-paragraph entry, I sent Yoani my efforts with a cover e-mail that, if I remember correctly, simply said, in this troublesome language, "Here."

Her succinct reply was the password to the English site. I immediately put a note in the sidebar—"This blog is the work of volunteer translators, please help us"—the plural "us" reflecting my optimism that help would come.

And it did. From an American student of Spanish who became my co-translator for many months, from a Cuban-Canadian, a Cuban-Spaniard with an American mother, an American who'd gone to Cuba in 1971 to cut sugar cane for Fidel's Ten Million Ton Harvest but who went now with cash stuffed in her bra to help young people escape, a Cuban-American with a degree in comparative literature, a college student in Miami whose father spent 14 years in Castro's prisons. Even my daughter helped out.

Soon the English site became a focal point for other languages, as volunteers from around the world filled my inbox: a retired psychiatrist in Brazil; an attorney in Amsterdam; a furniture-store owner in Japan; students in Portugal, Finland and Korea; a professor in Romania who set all his students to work: they all joined translators already working in Polish, German, French, and other languages.

As Yoani expanded the Cuban blogosphere, the translators were determined to support these new voices. An old friend and I worked to create a cooperative online translation site—HemosOido.com—where anyone can come and translate. In all, more than two hundred people have already helped spread the words of the Cuban bloggers around the world.

With the password to her website, Yoani also gave me the gift of her language, her island, her friends, and a network of people around the globe who believe that humans possess certain inalienable rights, one of which is to speak our minds freely and without fear.

To this day I have never met Yoani nor any of the other bloggers, and I have only met two of the translators. But I know about their lives, celebrate their graduations, congratulate them on their weddings, welcome their babies (and grandbabies) into the world, and am grateful for their friendships.

And I imagine a day in the not-too-distant future when we will all gather on Havana's Malecon and sit side-by-side on that seaside wall, laughing about how different everyone is from whatever it was we expected and sharing the joy of being together in a free Cuba ... all of us brought together by the promise that Yoani made to herself just a few years ago: To live—in Cuba—as a free person.

M.J. Porter, 2011

★

I approach the keyboard of my old laptop—sold to me six months ago by a rafter who needed money to buy an engine—and start writing. The rafter's journey failed, but the computer belongs to me, so there is no turning back now. I start with something halfway between a scream and a question, unsure if this will be my first post, the original entry of a blog. The scene is simple: A weak woman, without dreams, sits down to describe what is not reflected on the boring TV or in tedious national newspapers.

Before I begin my disillusioned vignettes of reality, the voice of apathy warns that my writing won't change a thing. The whisper of fear reminds me that I have a twelve-year-old son and warns me of the damage I could do to his future. I hear the voice of my mother saying, "Oh sweetheart, why do you want to get involved in that?" I anticipate being called a puppet of the CIA or an agent for State Security. The guard inside my head is rarely wrong, but the crazy person who shares that space won't listen to her. So, I start circling around my first post, and with it, the empty shopping bag, the tall, useless ministry buildings, the gnawing hunger and the raft floating in the Gulf, all pass to another plane.

I've only written a few lines, but now I am a blogger. I have the vertigo of someone who has just appointed herself publisher and editor-in-chief. It's only been a few months since I first read a blog; it was written by a countryman under the pseudonym "a

Cuban of the Island." His stories are so like my life, I have the sense he is my next-door neighbor. But no, he's a member of the Communist Party—one whose usual literary form is the official report denouncing illegal traders.

I christen my new space Generation Y, a blog inspired by people like me, people with names that begin or contain a "Greek Y," so unusual in Spanish. We are the generation born in Cuba in the seventies and eighties, marked by Schools in the Countryside, Russian cartoons, illegal emigration and frustration. So I especially invite Yanisleidi, Yoandri, Yusimi, Yuniesky and all the others who drag their "Greek Y," to join me and to write to me.

In those decades that were so tightly controlled, one small area of freedom was left unsupervised: the simple act of naming children. Thus our parents—hemmed in on every side, all wearing the same rationed pants or blouses—asserted themselves by giving their children these exotic "Y" names. Though we are a diverse group, we all share our Hellenic letter. Our ranks range from political police interrogators to prostitutes chasing tourist dollars. But a thread of cynicism binds us all, the cynicism necessary to live in a society that has outlived its dreams, and seen the future already exhausted before we got there.

We with "Y" names reached puberty as the Berlin wall came down, and the Soviet Union was just the name of a colorful magazine, dust-covered in kiosks. Without aspiring to utopias, our generation is firmly planted on the ground, inoculated against social dreams.

I post my first texts on the Internet. And together with the rest of the virtual world, they create a framework: a framework of marginal notes, from Cuba, at the beginning of the millennium. These notes—this raft made of binary code—begins to form a picture.

Three years after my first tentative filing there are more than five hundred posts—some of which I have tried to compress in this book. And there are nearly a million reader comments converting my private, cathartic space into a public square. Novels are already finished when they reach the page, but the Web, with its hypertexts, hot zones, and interactivity, has barely been touched in literature. Capturing this virtual world in the form of a book is so hard that I have given up trying.

So consider this book a companion to the blog; for the reader who wants more, or who wants to know what happens next, the blog is still there, online, growing like an enormous virtual beast, with more posts and more comments, and in twenty languages.

2007

★

Given a ration card at birth, and entering adolescence during Cuba's "Special Period," my thoughts are obsessed with food. I have to control myself not to let my desires run away with me, or to show the naked hunger that I see in the faces of my friends.

I look at them heading to the market with their plastic shopping bags, often returning with them just as empty as when they left. I, too, have a shopping bag, but I keep it folded in my pocket, so I don't look like I've been devoured by the machinery of the waiting line, the search for food, the gossip about whether the chicken has arrived at the market... In the end, I have the same obsession with getting food, but I try not to show it too much.

New status symbol

I live equidistant from two agricultural markets. In one, the sellers are either farmers or members of a cooperative farm, the other is run by the Youth Labor Army. In the first, there is nearly every fruit, vegetable, and other food, even pork, that one could want. In the second, the State market, there is rarely more than sweet potatoes, peppers, onions and green papayas. When there is some kind of meat, lines are longer. But the fundamental difference between the two markets is not variety but price—so much so that my neighbors call the farmers' market "the market of the rich" and the Youth Labor Army's market the "market of the poor."

The truth is, to serve a fairly balanced meal you have to go to both. First, you must inspect the plentiful stands in the large "market of the rich." Then you must review the capricious offerings and dubious quality in the "market of the poor."

Sometimes, overcome by desire and nostalgia, I buy a pineapple in the "market of the rich." But I take care to bring a cloth shopping bag to hide this queen of the fruits, this obscene symbol of status, from the jealous glances of others.

The children of waiting

I read a few days ago, in the newspaper *Granma*, that the Cuban population is shrinking and that there are 4,300 fewer inhabitants in 2006 than there were in 2005. The news does not surprise me. I had guessed that fewer students per class in the primary schools was due more to demographic reality than to a new teaching method.

Among my friends however, there is a real boom in pregnancies and births. These newborns are the children who had been postponed due to lack of living space, emigration, or the economic situation, but who their parents, already in their thirties, feel compelled to have now.

My friends imagined the arrival of their babies differently. They dreamed of solving their housing problems before bringing children into their lives. Some imagined that their children would go tobogganing and speak two languages, while others thought they would live in a country where their own salaries would allow them to afford disposable diapers, baby bottles, and Christmas gifts.

Life usually makes a mockery of our expectations. Here are my women friends, on the verge of giving birth or already rocking babies, while the fathers are suffocating, trying to subdivide the small space in their grandparents' homes, where they all live, and making calculations about what they can't afford on their meager wages. Meanwhile, they still dream that there will be a toboggan.

When I watch TV...

This week we are having anti-television therapy in our house. We started gradually, and now we only turn on the "smug little fatty" without the volume. This does something extremely interesting. Before our eyes pass images so predictable that our imaginations add voices and sound. If there is a seeded field, inside my head I hear a well-known commentator announcing overachievement in potato production. If we see images of people in white coats, my mind immediately hears the speech about Cuban doctors who offer their services in Bolivia or Venezuela.

When watching on mute, however, I never hear anything resembling actual conversations that I hear daily on the street. Our small screen shows us "what should have been" or, even worse, "what we must think we are." So, the commentator in all of us never says, "Prices are sky-high," "In my polyclinic we have only seventeen doctors because all the rest have left on a mission," "If you don't steal from your workplace you can't live," or "Where are the damned potatoes that never come?"

What I see on television bears so little resemblance to my life that I have come to think it is my life that isn't real; that the sad faces on the street are actors who deserve Oscars; that the hundreds of problems I navigate just to feed myself, get transportation, and simply exist are only lines in a dramatic script; that the truth, so adamant are they about it, must be what they tell me on the National Television News and the Roundtable talk show.

The gift of invisibility

For years I boasted that I could become "invisible." Because at any moment, I could immediately go undetected and escape from complicated situations. Wrapped in this "Harry Potter" cloak, I eluded the Union of Communist Youth, because—incredibly enough considering Cuba's ideological extremism in the 1980s—no one asked me if I'd like to join.

I was also invisible to any position of responsibility that required an unblemished record. Thus, I avoided, with hardly anyone noticing, until today, the almost obligatory enrollment in the Federation of Cuban Women; I simply played the old trick of having an identity card for one address but living in another. I also got around membership in a union. And I even managed to sidestep the "University is for Revolutionaries," as I was lucky enough to study at the School of Letters, during a time of relaxed bureaucracy due to the severe conditions of the Special Period.[1]

However, the hiding trick no longer works. So, I have "pointed myself out" with an act of extreme exhibitionism: Writing this blog. My friend told me the golden rule

he learned in a conversation with "the boys of the apparatus."[2] He said: "You can sign your own name to anything
you think and write, but you aren't allowed to *publish* any of
those things, particularly if you have signed them."

So, inspired by my friend's story, I got a little carried
away and put my picture up on this blog. Although I appre-
ciate the advice of those who have written in asking me to
please use a pseudonym and to take my photo down from
the site, I should tell you all that this is part of my "anti-
invisibility" therapy.

Similes, eternity, and power

I avoid using words such as "eternal," "always" and "never."
The definitive scares me and the everlasting stinks. When
I hear someone making a political speech saying, "its fire
will be as eternal as the Revolution," referring to the fragile
flame of a torch, I run to my dictionaries and calm my fright
with clear definitions of the words "ephemeral," "perish-
able," and "transitory."

It turns out that "eternal" is not only that which lasts
into the future *ad infinitum*, but that which has no beginning, which was always there. No one doubts the temporal
existence of the flame at Santa Ifigenia cemetery. It is clear
that once it did not exist and now it does. Why then this absurd parallelism, this demonstrably false simile, comparing
two transient things—fire and revolution—claiming that
each carries within it the seed of immortality?

At times, these phrases of permanence have such a
strong effect on me that I have to conjure up images of

the future. I see myself as an old woman telling my grand-children about everything we think of as eternal today. In return, I get from them the welcome thoughtlessness of the young, "Ah, Grandma, don't talk about *that* any more, everyone's already forgotten it. You go on and on about the same old thing."

It's a relief that all the things in this world's days are numbered.

And my glass of milk?

After Raúl Castro's televised speech of July 26, I ran into several friends who all greeted me in the same way. They all alluded to the "glass of milk" Castro had promised us in front of the cameras. From his entire, nearly sixty-minute panegyric, this is the one promise people remembered—which he announced like a victory achieved—"that every Cuban can drink" a glass of precious milk whenever he likes.

To me, someone who grew up on a gulp of orange-peel tea, the news seemed incredible. I believed we would put a man on the moon, take first place among all nations in the upcoming Olympics, or discover a vaccine for AIDS before we would put the forgotten morning *café con leche*, coffee with milk, within reach of every person on this island. I seem skeptical, I know. But those who edited Raúl's speech for the daily newspaper *Granma* must have felt skeptical too, because, in both the paper and online editions the promise of milk was cut.

Stubbornly, I sat in front of the television for the July 27 rebroadcast, to hear again about this conquest we were poised to make. My astonishment only doubled when, at the exact moment of the already unforgettable phrase, they cut away to a sea of flags and cheers on the Plaza Ignacio Agramonte.

At that point I didn't know if, in my food delirium, I had dreamed about that glass of milk, or if it really existed...

Metaphor for these times

This is the story of a building—Yugoslav model—that was built in the 1980s by excited *microbrigadistas*, all people who were building their own homes for the first time.[3] With their efforts came new experiences regarding ownership (very few in "Generation Y" have had such experiences). All of the builders had to work between four and seven years building their apartments and later had to make payments—which, after twenty years, gave them the opportunity to have title to the property.

This building reflects the story of these *microbrigadistas* who are now the owners of their own homes. They went from dreams of building—eager to have a place to live that was their own—to the frustrations of limited ownership in a half-finished property. What once was promised as a shining example of construction is now a modern ruin; a metaphor for the stagnation and decline of our times.

For the last four years no one has taken on the job of "manager" or "cleaner" here because fourteen floors, with long hallways and many stairs, are too much work for too little money. The elevator survives thanks to some residents who, in recent years, faced the dilemma of learning something about mechanics or taking the stairs. The water pump also has its own team of resident "water-pumpers" who repair it each time it breaks down. This self-management keeps the building from total collapse, but cannot stabilize its decline.

Proximity to the Plaza of the Revolution means that this fourteen-story apartment block is in a "frozen zone" where any vacancies fall into the hands of the Revolutionary Armed Forces (FAR) or the government. Window grates are proliferating, and some neighbors take turns cleaning the hallways of their floors or the small area in front of their own doors. The common areas suffer from the indifference of a form of ownership that does not make it clear who owns what. In theory, the common areas belong to everyone, but in reality this community of 144 apartments cannot decide what to do with them.

The residents are not allowed to open a needed coffee shop to raise funds to invest in the building itself. Also, they are forbidden access to a wholesaler to buy the hundreds of meters of pipe needed to fix the many leaks. The neighbors must wait and hope that the Institute of Housing will designate funds for the needed repairs.

Trapped in this bureaucratic nightmare, the *microbrigade* dreamers watch plaster fall, iron rust and paint fade. Their children are not interested in the saga of the construction or the assembly of the prefabricated parts. All that is an "old folks obsession." The young ones tease their parents when they tell the stories of the crane or the scaffolding: "So much sacrifice for this?"

The mottos of inaction

More and more often I hear, "Don't sweat it." It's repeated
every time someone challenges something he doesn't like.
The expression: "You'll give yourself a heart attack," "Just
ignore it," and "That's not going to accomplish anything,"
seem to be today's most popular phrases. A widespread call
to inaction, in the name of preserving mental hygiene, has
taken over Cubans' ability to act.

The person who complains or demands his rights is seen
as "some kind of weirdo." Meanwhile, others hide behind silence for fear of making trouble for themselves. Solidarity
is scarce if you protest having to wait in line, for example.
People fear losing the chance to buy something they have
waited so long for.

Ironically, often the person who prevents you from
speaking out then looks to you for complicity and silence.
This happened to me recently when I tried to use the Internet at the government-owned telephone company, ETECSA,
on Obispo Street. The official told me, "*Mami*, you know
very well I can't let you do that. Don't give me a hard time,
this is for tourists." The opportunistic voice of conformity
came, this time, from a woman in line waiting to pay her
phone bill: "Oh, honey, don't make problems, in the end it
won't change anything."

With all the calls "not to get upset," we Cubans have
come to believe that cardiac health conflicts with the demand for our rights, and that a stroke is the inevitable
outcome of demanding good service. I imagine enormous
billboards along the highway warning: "Criticizing, insist-
ing and demanding are bad for your health."

A few gray hairs, many dreams

August 22, 2007: Let me make a tribute in this blog to the journalist Reinaldo Escobar, who just turned sixty. It has been an enviable six decades of adventures that in a normal life would fill about two hundred years.

He worked as a journalist in the official media until he was expelled from the profession in 1988 because his articles "did not conform to the editorial line of the newspaper *Juventud Rebelde*." Then, in order to survive, he became an elevator mechanic. He faced the setbacks with the same wisdom with which he counsels many and is an adoptive father to hundreds. "This happens because we are living," he says, avoiding the ostracism, slander, and suspicions of many, not to mention visits from the "boys of the party apparatus."

Macho, as his friends call him, was born to a generation of troubadours, in the already mythical group "Macho Rico," which they became the last Friday of each month during the hardest years of the Special Period. On the hall table, a bowl of sugar welcomed anyone who, after climbing fourteen flights of stairs, needed energy to sing, read, or play the guitar.

Something of a spirit doctor, as his native Taíno features confirm, he has the enviable ability to explain almost everything. He is always ready to "stick his nose into it" on any project, and young people find that he suggests crazier and bolder ideas than anything they had in mind. Reinaldo Escobar collects friends, dictionaries, and projects, and he always reminds us that what is important "is not what happens to you, but how you handle it."

Macho, with whom I have shared my life and my projects for fourteen years, is an example, painful for many, of what can be reached with a few gray hairs and many dreams at age sixty.

Enjoy them, my love!

★

The summer of 2007 is at its height. Between eleven o'clock and three the street is sweltering. But hope is born when the media reports Fidel Castro's illness. If we had to hang onto a hot nail to believe in change, we would. Even if that nail is named Raúl Castro, seventy five-years-old, and partly responsible for the economic and social disasters of Cuba. These chronicles take their first steps amid this hope.

And I am not the only one waking from a trance that has kept me silent: the whole country is beginning to awaken. The man who tied the destiny of an entire nation to his own person has confessed that he is ill.

Now, the housewives seem calmer because the Brazilian soap operas run during prime time without the delays formerly caused by the Great Orator. The sportsteam coaches feel freer because they don't have to listen to his advice. The weathermen are still startled, however, in the middle of a hurricane, by the precise and irrefutable prognostications of the Expert-in-Chief.

The ministers, meanwhile, don't know if they will have to make their own decisions, or if Raúl Castro will inherit all the ministerial duties held by his brother. But all of them, to greater or lesser degree, feel an enormous olive-green weight lifted from their shoulders.

Without the dreaded finger pointing at all who trespass, my posts dare to go beyond what had been possible under the severe gaze of Fidel Castro. The vigilant "boys of the apparatus" are still dozing, perhaps thinking that the skinny girl who had opened this blog will abandon it before too long. A terrible calculation and a worse strategy on their part, concerning what will become a flood of commentators and journalists who turn Generation Y into a phenomenon that surprises us all.

The school year starts

For the first time this week, my son wore his mustard-colored uniform to the prefabricated Colonial-style high school barely five minutes from our apartment building. The last days of summer vacation were a process of buying shoes, searching for a new backpack, and discussing how much to narrow oversized pants.

The morning of the first day went by with passionate speeches and promises of a perfect course of study from the administration. Then came time for us to get familiar with this new-model high school, so different from the one I attended. Now, for instance, high school students are not allowed to go home for lunch. The rule is aimed at eradicating the difference between students who have a good lunch waiting for them at home and those who have less, or nothing, waiting for them. It is also aimed at preventing teenagers from wandering the streets and committing crimes.

Under this new system, at noon each student receives a sandwich of some protein food and a glass of yogurt. But at that age, the small portions only serve to whet a fierce appetite and make stomachs rumble during afternoon classes. So, at twenty past twelve, parents can be seen approaching the school fence with little bags, jars, and spoons to reinforce their child's diet. Some schools have banned the practice of bringing food to students, while other schools have announced that all students must bring their lunch in the morning.

Every day, in a quiet, stealthy way, I approach the school and pass a "shopping bag" through the fence with the necessary reinforcement. I see many parents doing the same, but I also see that a good share of the kids don't get additional food. So in the end, trying to erase differences has created a new one. It is a difference so visible and sad that I wonder if it wouldn't be better to be more flexible and allow youngsters to have lunch at home, while guaranteeing decent food for those who stay at school.

Everything that is imposed, mandatory, and rigid ends up being undermined, weakened, and rejected.

Under custody

What's going on? Should I be alarmed every time now when I see a huge police detail in the streets, especially in Central and Old Havana? Should I be alarmed seeing police on every corner, or seeing Central Park and the Capitol guarded by "black wasps" or "red berets" with dogs? Is it such an everyday occurrence that we aren't even amazed anymore?

We Cubans have seen our cities filled by these people who, deployed from Mercedes-Benz trucks, patrol in pairs, brandish clubs, and call us "citizens." It is common to have to show ID when walking with a friend from another country. Common that buses are stopped in the middle of the street and bags inspected to see if we are carrying some cheese, a lobster, or some dangerous shrimp hidden among our personal belongings.

The police presence, however, has not brought a decrease in crime, but rather a refinement in illegality. People have learned to evade them, to avoid the corners they watch, to more effectively mask cheese brought from another province.

Speak now or shut up until the next debate

Maybe it's just my desire to believe that something's changing that makes me notice a new tendency toward a collective catharsis. Where I once saw shrugged shoulders and people pretending not to see, I now see fingers pointed at problems and mouths disagreeing. Taking the first available opportunity—during a school assembly or in line to buy bread—tongues wag. Sharp words progressively dismantle what the media works harder every day to make us believe.

This wailing wall extends around the whole island. It is moved, in part, by Raúl Castro's call for deliberation in his July 26 speech, but mainly moved by exhaustion with the "cycle of silence" which has started to break down. Little by little, we are finding the satisfaction of speaking publicly about our problems. Gradually, we find joy in questioning the government, and the massiveness of the combined laments encourages us, so we grow bolder.

There is also a lot of skepticism from people who have

witnessed other periods of debate that came to nothing. "Remember the discussions prior to the fourth Cuban Communist Party Congress and the subsequent crackdown," say those who don't feel encouraged. However, I'd like to believe that what we are living is unstoppable. Those who have started to express dissatisfaction with small salaries, corruption, or the deterioration of the healthcare system will unavoidably come to question the political system, the authority to make decisions for all the people, and even issues of international relations.

Maybe it's purely my delusion, but it seems to me that what has started as a whisper is going to end in a scream.

Happy hearts

I promised myself I wouldn't be upset by the research of the scientists at the University of Cienfuegos showing the positive health effects of the Special Period. As statistics can prove almost anything, it's not worth attacking falsification of our low cholesterol levels. But looking in the mirror, seeing the obvious results in height and weight from those "tough years," I can't contain myself.

My generation lived through puberty marked by "there isn't any"—dreaming of the cans of condensed milk and Bulgarian canned food we enjoyed in the 1980s. We met to talk about food, while devouring tablespoons of sugar and nasty-tasting things of dubious origin that our parents prepared by making mountains of sacrifices. Food was an obsession that still marks us.

A study whose results measure only the low levels of fat

in our bodies is too superficial. Who will count the mental imbalances caused by those deprivations, the suicides, the escapes in improvised rafts to flee the empty plates, the personal and professional projects that remain unfinished, the children who were not born, the frustration, and the compulsion we still have to put anything we can into our mouths?

I would like to read the whole study for myself, and to look for places where, along with terms like "blood pressure," "sedentary lifestyle," "cholesterol," and "health," there are other words such as "happiness," "tranquility," and "dreams."

I suspect, you suspect, we all suspect

My son's teacher announced that among the students there is one—anonymous for now—who is on a list of those who misbehave. What these children are learning in school is the paralysis caused by the sense of being watched, the fear of provoking denunciation. For now, the whiff of being a delinquent can only result in scolding or punishment, but the day will come when it can cost a job, the ability to travel, small privileges won, or even one's freedom.

For those who have lived with suspicion and paranoia since childhood, trust is a feeling that only brings problems. We are all suspicious of everyone. We doubt the neighbor who smiles while looking at what we carry in our bags, the friend who visits at obviously strategic times, and the relative who talks nonsense on the telephone. We distrust those who leave, because they might be following orders from outside, and we guard our views here because criticism can be dangerous for the unwary.

I look around me and see that the repeated fertilization of our paranoia has worked. CIA agents and members of State Security populate our fears. The instilled fear of the "mole"—who could be anyone and from whom we must protect ourselves—is the most efficient trick, the most effective and successful path to disunity.

Time is worth nothing

I challenge you to find a public clock in this city that tells the time or at least an approximation of the real time. I cannot find one. Not even on the facade of the Train Terminal, where immobile hands always mark five twenty. It is not that we have some sort of aversion to gears or digital display, but rather that to us time is worth nothing.

We can spend an hour on line to pay the electricity bill or consume half a day to get a pair of shoes repaired. If, at the end of the day, we have completed at least one errand, that is reason enough to feel fortunate. Organizing or trying to make more efficient use of our time only leads to neurosis or masochism.

But what adventures every day! Not knowing exactly when we can take the bus, receive a service, or buy a ticket. Bless us that we do not care whether it is half past nine or ten fifteen. Those annoying instruments that attempt with their tick-tock to measure the passage of minutes and hours will only give us a bad conscience and steal from us the pleasure of the placid sensation of wasting time.

Those who don't show their faces

The film *The Lives of Others*, which will air December 8 at the Acapulco Cinema, will show the Cuban public scenes they already know well. This German film, a part of the Festival of the New Latin-American Cinema, will bring us a story that could well be that of a neighbor, or a friend, or our own story. It will confirm for us that the sensation of feeling ourselves observed is not a paranoid delirium, but clear evidence of a spy apparatus operating in the shadows.

Those who can get seats will identify, in the face and the attitude of Wiesler (the Stasi captain), the agents "Moises" or "Erick," "Carlos" or "Alejandro." They will understand that bugging telephone lines, filling a house with microphones, or blackmailing someone with his darkest perversions are techniques for which the restless boys of the Ministry of the Interior have no copyright.

I learned a long time ago that the best way to fool "security agents" is by making public everything one thinks. To sign our names, speak our opinions, and not hide anything disarms their dark maneuvers of vigilance. Let's save them, then, with our "guts in the open," from long hours of listening to recordings, from working undercover, from expensive gas for the cars they drive, and from long shifts searching the Internet for our divergent opinions.

We also know that our spies, the ones from here, are definitely not Germans: They neglect their work to watch the swinging hips of a girl passing by, they lose files, or they fall asleep while watching us through our windows. Nevertheless, they are similar to the German agents in their inability to show their faces, to say their real names, or to sign and publish all of what they whisper to us from the impunity of the shadows.

Open up!

I have posted a picture of the entrance to the Acapulco Cinema from last Saturday, December 8th, showing of *The Lives of Others*. I think it was the biggest mob I've seen at this festival. Outside we were yelling "Open up!" after they started closing the doors in response to the stampede of people who wanted in. I imagine that such a scream was not limited to the desire to enter the Acapulco Cinema, it was also a call to "Opening" with a capital "O." I, too, yelled it, thinking about the barriers, the limits, and the borders that must yield and let us through.

"Open up!" we yelled outside the cinema, and an hour later we could hear a character in the film saying, "The wall has fallen." "Open up!" we cried with faces against the glass, while they pushed us back. "Open up!" we continued thinking, even when we were already inside and seated in the comfy chairs, with the lights about to go off. "Open up!" They were the words that I kept from that night, and I repeated them the next morning.

The movie, renamed here *Our Lives*, allowed us to yell openly, right in the middle of 26th Street, a phrase that concentrates all of our desires: "Open up!"

Of TV classes and other absurdities

Teo, my son, doesn't belong to "Generation Y." Nevertheless

he is an endless source of anecdotes for this blog. His school stories generate smiles, worries and another post (which he is never interested in reading, because it is "old people's stuff"). Being up-to-date on what is said in his classroom, the music he dances to, and the words he invents connects me with those teenagers who someday will throw back in our faces all "this," which we are leaving to them.

A few weeks ago, Teo came home with geography home-work. "What are the portions into which Central America is divided?" asked his worksheet. Which led us to search our memories and the dictionaries. I tried to explain to Teo that in my school days, there were other categories such as "zones" or "areas" or "ecosystems," but not this word "por-tion" that reminds me more of a piece of pie than a stretch of land. So I asked him about the origin of such a novel cat-egory; his answer: "They said it on the tele-class."

For those who are not quite up-to-date with the "new educational methods" of Cuban middle school, I should explain that a TV in every classroom plays the role of the teacher about 60 percent of the time. Young people are bored, they can't say, "Teacher, please repeat, I didn't un-derstand," and they must copy without pause whatever is dictated from the screen. This new pedagogic technique is an attempt to alleviate the crisis in teachers caused by low salaries and little social or institutional recognition.

In doubt about "portions," I went to the school and asked a teacher (the flesh-and-blood one, not the virtual one on the screen) what this new geographic definition means. What I heard was already familiar: "Um, I don't know, they said that in the tele-classes." So I decided to sit down every morning at home to listen and take notes from the educational programs on TV. If I don't do it, how will I be able to help Teo with his questions?

It has now put me in the role of interpreting for my son the boring chit-chat of the "TV teacher." I even got a VHS tape, and tomorrow I will start recording the tele-classes!

Coming out of the closet

My friend Miguel, gay and dissident, is hopeful because new measures pushed by Mariela Castro will allow him access to sex-change surgery. He dreams of having an ID card with an identity that is "She" and not "He" and of being treated as the woman he feels himself to be. He knows, however, that he'll have to wait a lot longer to legally join a social-democratic party, to demonstrate in a picket line for his labor rights, or to vote, in direct elections, for another president.

With his new name, which for years he has decided will be Olivia, he won't be completely free from intolerance. Maybe he'll come to be accepted in his differences, as long as this is about his "sexual preference" and not his ideological tendencies. Coming out of the closet of his political opinions will take more time. And he will be reminded, in due course, that this Revolution allowed him to realize his dream of transsexuality.

I can't understand how we can invoke a tolerance that is parceled out and unfinished. How can we be on the cutting edge of gay-marriage reform and not be allowed, on the other hand, to "marry" another political point of view or social doctrine? All the thousands of Cubans locked in closets of double morality, repressing their true opinions, as if they were effeminate gestures, are waiting for a Mariela Castro to say publicly, "These too we must accept and tolerate in their difference." Miguel will then be the social-democratic woman he has always dreamed of being.

You too, Carlos?

We spent Tuesday with the phone ringing and friends coming over to talk about Carlos Otero, the best-known presenter on Cuban TV, who asked for asylum in the United States. This news has been the fastest-circulating word-of-mouth story in the last few months—perhaps because it concerns a man of the media. He was the only one, in all our sleepy TV programming, whose program carried his own name: "Carlos, period."

Accustomed as I am to seeing more of my friends leave each year, I was not surprised that this "man of success" chose exile. His decision is like that of many who understand that they have no future here, who have come to realize that Cuba is not a country where dreams can come true. I confirm this every time I ask my acquaintances about their plans for the future and I hear, more than half the time, "What I want is to leave." This answer grows alarmingly more frequent the younger the person is.

This continuous hemorrhaging, which every month takes away the youngest, the boldest and—why not say it?—the most talented, is proof that the well-being of the people is not a center of attention for the Cuban government.

Politics, ideology, and past evidence of loyalty are priori-
tized above the "here and now" of our needs. As long as the
"higher-ups" don't recognize that they haven't been able to
build a country where people want to stay and use their energies, the problem of emigration will not be solved.

How many will have to leave before we can hear the
phrase, "We failed, we haven't been able to give Cubans a
future"? I suspect, because I see the hardheadedness that
comes with too many years in power, that not even this
desolate postage stamp of an island, full of tired and aging people whose children live in other latitudes, will make
the Cuban government see reason. I can already hear the
accusations of "unpatriotic," "sell-out to imperialism" and
"traitor" that will be heard at the Institute of Radio and
Television when they hear about the self-exiled newscaster.

What they don't know is that with the exit of Carlos
Otero, those who stay behind feel that the island is increasingly empty and terribly boring.

An empty chair

Today I'll celebrate Christmas Eve with my family and
friends. We'll assemble an improvised table from the old
doors of the elevator and cover them with a blanket for
a tablecloth. Everyone will bring something to the party.
We won't have grapes, cider, or nougat candy—traditional
elements of a Cuban Christmas celebration—but we'll be
together in harmony, which is itself a great luxury. The children will have their government-guaranteed soft drinks,
while the adults will have a little rum with lemon or honey.

My mother will recount how hard it was to get tomatoes in the morning and my niece will remind us that on Tuesday the 25th she'll play a little angel in the mass at her parish.

At the head of the table, we'll place a chair that has remained unoccupied since Christmas 2003. It is a chair for Adolfo Fernández Saínz, condemned during the Black Spring to fifteen years in prison. It will be sad to see, for a fifth time, his absence.[4] If his jailers allow, we'll be able to hear his voice on the phone, cheering us up. (How ironic life is! He, who is in jail, has the strength to cheer us up.)

I remember when we told my son that he was in jail. My husband told him: "Teo, your uncle Adolfo is in jail because he's a very brave man," to which my son replied with his innocent logic: "Then you are free because you're a little bit cowardly." What a direct way of telling the truth children have! Yes, Teo, you are right. This Christmas we warm our chairs because we are "cowards." We wish, in the privacy of our family, for a new year of liberty, but we can't make those wishes a reality. We content ourselves with the myth of national destiny, because we have given up on acting to change things.

Adolfo's empty chair will be the freest territory at our improvised Christmas table.

Do we arrive or not?

The feeling of a string pulled taut, of collective asphyxiation, is the feeling in the streets. This is a strange December. I don't hear anyone making predictions for the new year. Not even the timid prediction that 2008 might bring us "better things." We spent those hopes last New Year's Eve, when we speculated that in 2007 the desired economic openings and the needed political changes would come.

By the end of July, it was clear that things were going a lot more slowly than we had hoped. And now, in the last weeks of December, we believe that the "higher-ups" are "buying time." Announcements promise us drinking water available all day, repaired roads, and new buses circling the city. It all reminds me of the promised goals of forty or fifty years ago. How limited, late, and false they seem to me now.

So, lacking announcements of resolutions or hopes, I am going to make my own—a simple and clear list of desires for this leap year. Heading the list will be that, by next December, we won't have this sensation of "another year gone by without bringing us what we so greatly desire."

Happy 2008!

2008

A day without the black market

I try to imagine an incredible twenty-four hours in which I wouldn't have to rely on the black market. What about a day without the milk brought by those who knock at my door? They fill the absence of dairy products at the rationed market for those of us older than seven and younger than sixty-five. I can't conceive of a day without going to the black market to buy eggs, cooking oil, or tomato paste. Even to buy peanuts, I must cross the line into illegality.

If I'm in a hurry to get somewhere, most likely I'll have to take an unlicensed taxi. Not to mention the wide range of underground workers I must go to when my washing machine breaks, the gas oven clogs, or the shower stops working. All of them, in the shadows, sustain me day-to-day and supplement the limited services offered by the State.

Even the newspapers I buy, overpriced, come from the seniors who wake at dawn and buy up all the copies of *Granma* and *Juventud Rebelde* to resell to supplement their meager pensions. And we won't even talk about the "unmentionables" provided by the black market or the many "open Sesames" you get by slipping a bill into the right hands. But most surprising is the vendors' seemingly infinite capacity to regenerate after each of the many raids against them.

I don't know about you, but me, I can't live a day without the black market.

The Wishing Tree

People start arriving before seven in the morning. There we find everyone: the dreamers, the disillusioned, even the provocateurs. They wait under a tree, perhaps one of the flamboyant trees, on the side of the Central Committee building. They are there because they wish to present their letters, repeat their request or check, for the umpteenth time, to see if their pleas have had any effect. Some of them, from coming so often, know how to interpret the guard's gesture telling them they can go in. At the guard station they show their identity cards, and inside, behind the bulletproof glass, a man takes their papers and gives back a receipt.

An appeal to the "highest authorities" is the hope of all who wait there. Many have traveled hundreds of kilometers for this last chance. They believe that when the "high leaders" learn of their problems, the problems will be speedily solved. Under the Wishing Tree it is common to hear: "This happened to me because Fidel doesn't know about it. If he knew, for sure he would solve it." With similar dreams, they wait to be called into the building.

The lady in red pants is here because her house fell down twelve years ago and she lives in a shelter; the old man with the shattered voice demands a pension, snatched from him by bureaucracy and inefficiency; a young woman claims that her boyfriend is in prison even though he's innocent.

There's even a man hunkered down in the grass who seems to be, like me, from the group of skeptics.

The scene repeats itself every morning, Monday to Friday. Sometimes they raise their voices, mothers bring their kids to beg as a family, and someone appeals for calm saying, "Hey guys, shut up and wait, 'cause if you don't, you won't get anything."

On my way home I can see the Wishing Tree, each time projecting its shadow over more and more people. Every day, it is more bent under the weight of problems.

Hidden energies

I remember when, in 1994, they allowed licenses to open private restaurants, known as *paladars*. Havana filled with improvised kiosks that brought back lost flavors and recipes. Within a couple of months, the creativity flowered under hundreds of umbrellas, tables on porches, and even sophisticated spots where you could try a mamey shake or guava pie. Pent-up energies of thousands of Cubans were demonstrated in products and services of a quality and efficiency previously unknown by my generation.

We witnessed, with astonishment and happiness, the rebirth of small private enterprises that our parents had seen drowned in the Revolutionary Offensive of 1968. A stroll along the streets of Central Havana confirmed that the previous scarcity hadn't been born of an incapacity to produce, but rather from ironclad State controls on private ingenuity.

We ultimately had to say good-bye to this boom in

creativity and ingenuity, the moment the "higher-ups" came to understand that economic freedom would imply, inevitably, political autonomy. When Cuco, owner of the most famous *paladar* in my neighborhood, wanted to invest his profits in a trip to Paris, a modern car, and the creation of a "gastronomic" magazine, he began to worry the higher powers. In order to counter these "bourgeois poses" he was swamped with high taxes, controls, and a growing list of prohibitions. He had to close his restaurant, and the flavor delights we had rediscovered receded, again, into the shadows.

The "small private businesses" that survived the return to centralization reveal that all of those energies to produce are just waiting for restrictions to loosen to once again conquer our streets and porches. Cuco caresses his recipe book, expanded during these years of waiting, and plans a new restaurant on the roof of his house. He already has the design for his Web page, his presentation card and the color of the napkins. He is waiting at the starting line to begin the race that will allow him to compete for his dream.

Kids

For certain older people the carefree attitude of the young produces burning and regret. They intuit that those who follow them will wash away everything that they consider "holy." They are right. Nothing is more fearsome than a teenager who wastes his time and threatens to "change everything." And these are the seniors who, at the first opportunity, throw back in their grandchildren's faces the education offered, the diapers washed, the breakfasts served, even the medicines bought.

That rancor can be seen in the dismissive term "*joven-zuelo*"—kids—that Fidel Castro used in his penultimate "Reflections" column in the daily paper. The broadside attack on "*jovenzuelo*" started when a young Cuban (maybe a Yuniesky, Yohandry, or Yasiel) was interviewed by the foreign press and declared that he didn't want to talk about socialism. Showing the determination typical of the young, he drew a virulent reaction from the Head of State himself, who dedicated almost a paragraph to him.

The whole story of the fed-up youngster and the severe "grandpa's" reproaches transported me back to the years of *glasnost* and to the magazine *Novelties from Moscow*, in which a young man warned the sixty-somethings who were blocking the changes: "You have all the power, we have all the time." Of course, we have to temper that phrase, knowing that even for Yuniesky or Yohandry the years pass, and every day they have less time.

I have the hunch that I'll be a rather punk old lady. I'll allow the kids of 2050 to make fun of my pictures and the ugly hairdo that I've had for more than three decades. I'll let them tear down, one by one, everything that for me now is "untouchable." I'll do it gladly and approvingly, because I know that not only do they have the time, but they also inherit the power. A huge power that allows them to choose between "waiting or doing something."

Habeas data

I saw the images of the fall of the Berlin Wall for the first time eleven years after the events of that October 1989. At the time, few Cubans had access to a video player or to the foreign press. The news came to us when it was already history. The young man who defied a tank in Tiananmen Square only took shape before my eyes a decade after the incident happened. Not to mention things in Cuba that we barely heard about. Like when the *Maleconazo*—the riot along Havana's Malecon—happened in August 1994; we had to reconstruct the scene of sticks and stones from fragments on foreign television.

Gone are the days when the official newspapers, radio, or television are our only sources of information, or disinformation. Technology has come to our aid. Now, in spite of all the limitations on accessing the Internet, watching television via satellite dishes, or listening, without interference, to shortwave radio, news reaches us.

Excellent proof of this has been the rapid underground spread of the video of Eliécer Avila, a student at the University of Computer Sciences (UCI), who publicly questioned the president of the Cuban parliament. How the recording of those awkward questions was leaked—questions that made Ricardo Alarcon sweat, gesticulate wildly, and draw constant comparisons to the past—is the subject of speculation. But within just a few weeks, a good number of Cubans had seen or heard of that singular encounter.

It seems impossible to dismantle this fragile, clandestine network that brings us "news of ourselves." Biased, omitted, or distorted information has turned us into agile dredgers of data, masters of the art of digging up details. Today there is the video of Eliécer Avila at the UCI, tomorrow there will be more classified information that will spread through Cuban society.

While the official media maintains its bucolic lethargy, we are learning. The young man of UCI now has a face, we know his voice, we heard his opponent stutter. This is not some enormous square in China where a young man faces down tanks; this image will not take a decade to reach us.

By candlelight

February 19, 2008: I haven't been able to sleep since three o'clock this morning. The phone started ringing within minutes of Fidel Castro's latest posting on the newspaper *Granma* saying he is stepping down. From that moment on I could not go back to bed. It is difficult to think clearly when you get up before dawn, so I am still at the "pinch me to see if I'm awake" stage. My friends aren't much help, waking me up, harassing me with questions, as if anyone on this island might have "answers."

All of my life I have had the same president. And not just me, my mom and dad—born in 1957 and 1954, respectively—don't remember anyone but the man who just resigned.

Several generations of Cubans have never asked who will govern them. Nor do we have many doubts about who will now. But at least someone appears to be ruled out, once and for all. With only five days before the elections we have learned that our well-disciplined parliamentarians will face a different ballot. They will not have to check off the "same" candidate.

Despite being asleep on my feet, I realize that today is the end of a cycle. It is worth asking: Will the new president follow our desires, or will we wait another fifty years?

For the moment I close my eyes. I already feel much lighter.

Cow suicide

Our unique reality is a help in the writing of literature. Each small detail of our daily lives breathes fantasy, fiction, and paradox. Reading stories such as *Male Heifers and Other Absurdities,* by Ángel Pérez Cuza, is a walk through the injustices of every day. We understand perfectly when one of the characters tells us that "Brave Bull and Stud Ox are cows even if they have bulls' names," because it's a trick farmers use to get around the requirement to sell all milk to the State.

The issue of beef is one of the most surreal in Cuba today. This animal with udders and horns is as sacred here as it is in India. If, in that country, the motives are magical-religious, on this little island in the Caribbean the "cult of beef" is bureaucratic. Thus, we Cubans can read a paragraph like the following without surprise:

Do you know how long it's been since I've tasted beef? No? Me neither. And I could, because I have cattle and I can still breed Mazorra and Josefina. But I can't slaughter my animals. If one is sick or hurt, I must call the Plan to send out a veterinarian and an inspector. Butcher it to eat? Absolutely not! It must be cremated, with the proper papers and everything. Worse still if it is calving. It's a total mess. Complete investigation, experts from the police.

Reading this story by Pérez Cuza reminds me of an anecdote from more than twenty years ago. My father was a train conductor back in the eighties. I used to ride with him in the Soviet locomotive he drove. One day, from the driver's seat, I saw something move on the line about a hundred meters ahead. It was a cow, tied up in such a way that only its head was on the tracks. The animal mooed and tried to break loose but couldn't do it. With all the innocence of my ten years I yelled, "Papa, stop! There's a cow tied up on the line!" But a train with thirty cars doesn't stop easily, much less for an animal. My father, who had seen worse things on the iron track, calmly said, "Don't worry. The owners themselves tied it there so the train would kill it and they can eat it. Only when I run over her can they enjoy their meat." A few seconds later the sharp blow confirmed that the sacrifice had been made. Looking out the window, I saw a mob of smiling *guajiros* run toward the corpse.

I suppose in the two decades that have passed since this "suicide" Cubans have become more skilled at tying their cows to the rails. And Pérez Cuza has a lot of material for his stories.

On reprimands and "punctured" pages

I confess I have been given to misbehaving. I rebel against orders. I look for lemons that I can't find anywhere, I demand apologies that never come, and, this great silliness of mine, I write my opinions in a blog, with my name and picture attached. As you can see, in these thirty-two years—such impertinence—I'm due for my comeuppance.

So, the anonymous censors of our impoverished cyber-space want to send me to my room, turn off the lights, and not allow my friends to visit. Which means, in terms of the Web: blocking my site, filtering my page, and finally, "puncturing" my blog so my compatriots can't read it. For a couple of days now, *Generation Y* has been just an error message on the screen of Cuban computers—another blocked site for the "monitored" Internet users of the island.

My posts, and those of other bloggers and digital journalists, have caused the inquisitors to undertake this ridiculous task. With our haughty air of rebellious adolescence, we have earned a slap, a harsh stare, and a scolding. The reprimand, however, is so futile that it's pitiful, and it's so easy to get around that it becomes an incentive.

I can't believe it!

April 4, 2008: The part of me that still remembers my Philology—that remembers the names of writers, philosophers and scholars—is jumping for joy over receiving the Ortega y Gasset Prize for Journalism. And the blogger part of me feels that overcoming the many obstacles to accessing the Internet, so much flash memory spirited from here to there, has been worth all the effort.

I remember that it was April—T.S. Eliot's cruelest month—and I had decided to exorcise my demons through a blog. I began by casting out the most paralyzing things, the things that make the mask of silence so appealing. Secondly, I cast out the apathy that says not much can be done. And by mid-August, frustration, disenchantment, and doubts were already draining away with each new post.

What started as my personal therapy, to rid myself of all these aches and pains, has become a space for many who, by curious coincidence, had demons of their own.

Readers, I am only the face in the sidebar of the site. You—controversial and incendiary, censors and boycotters—are, at the end of the day, those who make the blog.

Exit or travel

I am working on a new university career, unrelated to any specialty. I am earning a "Bachelor of Circumventing the Bureaucracy." The subject studied is the formalities and papers required for travel outside Cuba; the assignments involve a good dose of patience, meekness, and mystery. I don't come empty-handed to this crash course in "paperwork." I drag a decade of experience in the turmoil of procedures. There are also the multiple scuffles with officials and a slow acceptance of the bad smells in the offices.

The experience of talking with bureaucrats—for those of us who always lack a document, a stamp, or a signature—will allow me to finagle the highest grade in this area. Nevertheless, I will have to overcome a certain predisposition to rage, an inconvenient fury, when I am told, "Your paper has not come in time," or, "It has to be approved by the higher-ups."

The end result of these exercises will be a small white card that authorizes me to leave Cuba to collect the Ortega y Gasset prize. I stress that I am not trying to "travel," as no Cuban uses this verb for the action of going abroad. We skip, cross, leave or go; but "travel" is too small a word for leaping over this bureaucracy. Even the long-awaited approval I need is known as an "exit permit" and carries with it the sound of locks clicking open.

I don't know how many hours I've accumulated in lines—the legal birth certificates, the requiring of documents that aren't needed, like my vaccination card and the latest electricity bill. I don't know, but I have the feeling that the answer to my travel request has already been decided and waits for me in a drawer. Nothing I can do could affect whether the key opens or closes the door. In the interim, I believe that "exit" is still possible.

Incubating mediocrity

In my son's middle school we had a parent meeting that lasted almost three hours and nearly ended in a fight.

The central school director read the Ministry of Education Resolution 177, approved last December, which establishes that academic ability will not be the determining factor when it comes time for students to pursue higher education. The students with the best grades will not be awarded the best seats in high schools of science or the arts, or in the technical schools of information technology and communications. Instead, the selection will reward students who are most "comprehensive."

The well-known criteria, based on grades received during middle school, have ceased to exist. In their place, teachers now have the power to determine—that is, pull strings for—which students excel in the new requirements. According to the new grading system, the following defines a "comprehensive" young person:

1. Attendance and punctuality
2. Attitude toward work
3. Attitude toward study
4. Discipline
5. Appropriately wears the uniform and demonstrates the attributes of a Pioneer
6. Participates in demonstrations and political/patriotic activities
7. Participates in cultural and sports activities
8. Cares for society and the environment
9. Human relations

Number six was enough to set off the alarms, as it provides fertile ground for opportunism and fakery.

This disturbing meeting occurred at the same time as latest Congress of the Cuban Writers and Artists Union, where several delegates criticized the Cuban education system and its formation of values. On the one hand, there is a demand to encourage talent and creativity, and on the other, the limits of an iron ideology which segregate those who think differently.

I do not worry too much for my son because it is two years before he moves up to high school and it is possible that this unpopular measure will no longer exist. However, I fear for a nation that unconditionally rewards ideology rather than talent; where a student who participates in a political demonstration can be graded higher than one who masters his subjects; where educational institutions teach students that the way to succeed is to dissemble.

What am I doing there?

Time Magazine has included me, along with ninety-nine famous people, in their list of the most influential people of 2008. As for me, I have never appeared on stage or mounted a podium, and even my own neighbors don't know if "Yoani" is written with an intermediate "H" or a final "S." I am even more surprised to appear under the heading "Heroes and Pioneers," and would prefer the simple title of "citizen."

Of the innumerable ways to reach that famous list, I believe I have traveled—by foot—the most unusual. One not shored up by economic power, charisma in front of the cameras, political control, or religious ancestry. I have simply devoted myself to telling my reality through a distorted focus of emotions and questions. I have come to believe that the voice of an individual can push back the walls, contradict the slogans, and fade the myths. Now, vanity alone overtakes me to imagine that others on the list are asking themselves, "Who is this unknown Cuban blogger who is among us?"

The fear of setback

Elsa bought a new DVD player and an electric pressure cooker. But her husband warns her to wait a bit for a mobile phone. He, who has seen things that made him shudder, still remembers "operation home appliance" of the nineties. On that occasion, his sister was accused of "illicit enrichment," and two air conditioners, a car, and some appliances were confiscated. So he advises his wife not to get too carried away with consumption.

In his paranoia he speculates about alleged lists of names of those who buy the new articles that appear on the market. For better or worse, Elsa purchases every new object in the name of a different family member. So, their seven-year-old daughter is legally the owner of the pot, while the twelve-year-old son holds title to the DVD player. The name of the grandfather, who can barely hear, will be on the contract for the cellular phone, if they decide to buy it. And it must never appear that they are accumulating more products than they can afford on their wages.

The caution is not unique to Elsa and her suspicious husband, but extends to farmers who fear that the land the government offered for their use will be re-nationalized once they free it of the invasive marabou weed and make it productive. Also, those who would like to go to a hotel are wary that permission for local citizens to enter these places might be reversed at any time.

The understandable fear of setbacks keep us in suspense before each new announcement. Anyone might think that this is an excess of suspicion on our part, but the record speaks for itself. The more prudent wait for the dreaded rectification, while the unwary are swept along by the rapture of the changes.

The capital of all Cubans?

I have twenty minutes to get to Central Park, to a small gallery near Plaza Vieja where a friend is going to talk about his paintings. If I walk I'll miss the beginning of the talk and the young painter won't forgive me. I grab a bicycle taxi and offer the cyclist ten pesos to go as fast as possible. He looks at me with joy because of how few pounds he will have to carry, and hums a reggaeton that goes: "I like the bat of the baseball player's wife, I like the meat of the butcher's wife, and the fireman's wife is asking me to the fire..."

Once underway I feel like a matron reclining in my palanquin. It lightens my guilt to think that if he were not carrying me, the poor driver would have had to pedal a fat couple who also tried to flag him down. But I'm still wrapped in my guilt, when the driver turns and asks: "Are you from Havana?" Yes, I tell him. With greedy eyes, he says, "I am from Guantánamo. I am looking for someone to marry me so I can get a Havana identity card. Are you single?"

The directness of the proposal unnerves me. I want to explain that I already have a partner, and I don't own a house where he can be registered and thus saved from deportation. It occurs to me to tell him that my neighborhood is very close to that tower—shaped like a truncated lollipop—which is home to Power, making it extremely complicated to house a new person. All the explanations about why I can't agree to his proposal are contained in one brief statement, "I can't."

The man looks at me as if I were condemning him to detention in the center for "illegals" we just passed—where buses depart each week expelling those who are "without papers" from Havana. His gaze makes me feel guilty for having been born in this dilapidated and exclusionary city, one that flirts with international tourists and disdains its fellow countrymen.

I am about to change my mind and marry him, but we arrive at the exhibition and my friend the painter saves me from the wedding ring.

Mother's Day, or "An Up-to-Date Mother"

My son is becoming a man and already demands his own space. For now, his territory is small: one room, the chaos of someone who cares little about the tedious ordering of possessions; and the anarchic slogan, "I want to do as I please." I can already predict clashes when his demands for autonomy will spread to his city and country. When the victory now achieved by hanging his icons on the wall grows into the desire to express some "uncomfortable" preference.

The day will arrive when hair, fashion, and music will not be enough to let him feel different. Then will come the agitator, reactionary, or extremist—with the absolute complicity of his progenitor. I promise you. It will not occur to me to banish him from the house, betray his actions, renounce his activities, or declare, to hide my own responsibility, that "I didn't raise him to be like that."

After all, he too has also had to put up with me. Whatever he may be: an eccentric, a pyromaniac, a protester, even
indifferent, I will stand beside him. You will have to ask him
if he will do the same for me, if one day this blog, my history, my excesses, will not weigh too heavily on his life.

Denunciation—Plea—Confession

They warn me that on a table in some office is "my case." A
file full of infractions, a bulky dossier of the illegalities I
have accumulated over the years. The neighbors hint that
I should disguise myself with sunglasses, disconnect the
phone, be wary when I talk about something private.

Soon, very soon, they warn me, you could hear a knock
at your door very early in the morning.

In anticipation of this, I would like to point out that I
do not keep weapons under the bed. However, I have in-
deed committed an unfailingly heinous offense: I have believed myself to be free. Nor do I have a firm plan to change
things, but for me complaint has replaced triumphalism
and that is definitely a punishable offense.

I've never slapped anyone, and I refuse to accept the
systematic swatting at my "rights as a citizen." This is
highly reprehensible. And, though I have never stolen anything from others, they want to "steal" again and again,
that which I believe belongs to me: an island, its dreams,
its legacy.

Don't get me wrong, I'm not entirely innocent. I carry
with me a mountain of misdeeds: I have routinely bought on
the black market; I have criticized, in a whisper, those who

govern us; I have nicknamed politicians and I have agreed with pessimists. To top it off, I have committed the abominable offence of believing in a future without "them" and in a different version of history than what I was taught. I repeated their slogans without conviction, washed dirty laundry in full view and—the greatest transgression—joined together words and phrases without their permission.

I confess, and accept the punishment for it. I cannot both survive and comply with their law, at the same time.

Happy peasants

With a few cans of meat, some candles and an old camera in their backpacks, the couple went to Santiago de Cuba by train and into the mountains early one Saturday morning. They wanted to walk to Baracoa, camp out in the mountain wilderness, make love in cabins with the boldness of sixteen-year-olds. The boy figured it would take them four days on foot to arrive in the first village founded in Cuba.

After the first night they saw a peasant leading a line of mules. The boy won the debate about whether to approach him or not: "Let's ask him for directions to the nearest cabin." The girl, more prudent, warned him that the mountains were not as they once were, that the country people shared little with outsiders. Nevertheless, they went up to the peasant, who cried out, "What are you doing here? You can't be on these mountains without government permission."

It was already too late to fix their mistake. They had to go with the man to the nearest town, where they would regret having asked their question. The principal of a one-room schoolhouse told them they would have to remain calm until the police arrived. He insisted in finding out where they got the idea to enter the Sierra Maestra Mountains. She spoke of Zen, cosmic energy, and t'ai chi exercises connecting her with nature. Neither the peasant nor the policeman believed her.

That night the regional manager arrived, and the couple had to repeat their story—they only wanted to go on a hike, camp together among the trees, and see Baracoa. They were taken to the police station in Santiago and put on a bus back to Havana. During the long journey back, they could not stop thinking about those inhabitants of a lost nation who had called the police. "Arrest them. They are going on a strange walk. Who would want to hike in these mountains?"

New rise in prices

Two weeks ago Marta's tiny pension was increased by thirty-five Cuban pesos. Waiting in line at the bank she ran into a friend who warned, "Watch out, now comes the rise in prices!" But, thinking her friend just another pessimist and naysayer, she didn't believe this alarming forecast. Big mistake. Because when she went shopping on Saturday she noticed that she needed more money to buy her staples in the shops that sell in CUCs, convertible pesos (worth roughly 25 Cuban pesos each, or one US dollar).[5]

Marta is sixty-two, and nothing surprises her. However, she got quite a scare when she saw that a bottle of cooking oil that used to cost 1.90 CUC—about 45 Cuban pesos—now costs 2.30 CUC. She didn't remember a single official

announcement about price increases, and she could have
sworn that people were expecting prices to drop. So the
"generous" increase in her retirement pay was just enough
to buy a little box of soup concentrate and a 300-gram bag
of detergent, the latter now costing 1.30 CUC, 30 percent
more than it did last week.

Much to her regret, the next time she sees her friend
she will have to admit she was right. Increases in salary are
tied to proportionate increases in prices.

Parallel worlds

May 31, 2008, 5:00 p.m. I'm at the door of the Café Cantante
at the National Theatre. The program doesn't interest me
much, but I came with a friend who is crazy about dancing.

5:27 p.m. The doorman asks for our institutional affiliation. Tables for nationals have been reserved for a group
of outstanding accountants. I explain that we are "indepen-
dents," and instead of being upset, he roars with laughter
and lets us in.

6:10 p.m. A screen plays video clips from the United
States, while the bar serves beer, rum, and soft drinks, sold
for convertible pesos. My friend and I are cornered by some
young men dancing lasciviously in tight-fitting clothes.
When they hear us speaking "Cuban" they take fright and
leave.

7:00 p.m. The recorded music continues. It seems the
band doesn't want to play or one of their members hasn't
shown up yet. The boys next to us are fidgeting in front
of three Spanish women who have just appeared. Each is

wearing something white; with the disco lights it's a strik-
ing effect.

7:40 p.m. Nobody else has approached our table, which
is strange considering we are two single women in a nightclub. Nationality seems to determine approachability.

8:20 p.m. Nothing about the ambiance here—young
guys who wink at women twice their age; sequins and designer clothes everywhere; and the general flutter about
every foreigner who enters—reminds me of the slogans of
austerity, ideological firmness, and discipline that swarm
outside.

8:40 p.m. The café, about to close, is across the street
from the tall ministry buildings that crowd this area. I cannot shake the feeling of two parallel worlds—worlds that
emphatically negate each other's existence.

9:00 p.m. As I leave, I see the boys with the white
clothes leaving with the women with the "zeta" accents. On
my way home I stumble upon the huge billboard alongside
the Council of State, from which José Martí warns, "One
should become in any given moment, that which is needed
in that moment."

We vote for humor

I act as the tongue of you, tied in your mouth,
in mine it begins to be loosen'd.
    —WALT WHITMAN

The character Chicken Brain convulses us with laughter
every Wednesday, on the show *Let Me Tell You*. This quick

"teacher" says on prime-time Cubavisión what we whisper in the streets. He can do it, even though he's in front of the cameras, because jokes and metaphor protect him. Still, at times his critiques are so clear and direct that from our living rooms we worry about the actor who plays the part. We are grateful that he makes fun of our absurd daily life, that he manages to show us what our own parliamentarians dare not speak of when they meet. Chicken Brain is the only public figure who represents my demands. But with all the mocking and fooling around, does he go too far?

Last Thursday I met several friends who said, "They are about to cut the program *Let Me Tell You*. They are criticizing it very strongly..." But the honorable and very wise Doctor Chicken Brain and his colleagues only put into the language of jest what we say every day. For example, he predicted the dismay of future archeologists when they find the remains of a chicken from our time. It will be difficult for them to reconstruct this animal, which regardless of whether it shows up in the ration stores or is sold for convertible pesos, never has a breast.

The characters Chicken Brain, Incompetent Lindoro, the Left Screw Workshop, and Dummy Perez say more about our reality and our doubts than the national news, the *Roundtable*, and all the TV analysts put together.

Evoking the Russians

Reading the *The Seventh Secretary* by Michel Heller brought back a flood of memories of the "Soviet phase" on this little island. I was not yet fifteen years old, but I have strong sensory memories of this colonial period. I recall the sweets and foods purchased through the informal markets run by the wives of Soviet technicians. Curiously, we never referred to them as Soviets, much less as "comrades." They were *"los bolos"* (the bowling pins), meaning unformed, coarse, unworked pieces of clay, massive and without grace, makers of washing machines that used the electricity of the entire house, but that—even today—continue to function.

Many of our parents had studied or worked in the USSR, but we knew nothing of borscht nor did we like vodka, and everything "Soviet" seemed old-fashioned, rigid, and passé. What paralyzed us about them was the bear-like power emanating from their gestures and the veiled warning with which they sustained our Caribbean "paradise."

The mixture of fear and mockery that *los bolos* generated in us still remains. If, today, a tourist does not want to be bothered by a persistent seller of tobacco, sex or rum, he only has to whisper *Tovarich* (comrade), or *niet ponimayu* (I don't understand), and the startled seller will melt away.

Four Roads but only one direction

The vast yellow-and-red market on Mount Street resembles a cloister now, rather than a crowded marketplace for fruits and vegetables. A police operation eliminated all the illegal vendors who had filled its stands and established order in a place where it used to be easy to lose your wallet. They are making essential repairs that may take half a year, or may take a decade.

Despite the former chaos of the Four Roads Market, it

was the best-stocked farmer's market in the city. I found
lemons there after several weeks of looking for them and—
once a month—I was able to replenish my supply of peanuts. Exotic ginger and the nearly-extinct soursop adorned
the stalls. Sometimes the market surprised us with the lost
flavors of star apple and egg fruit. It was a veritable museum of what was once produced by this island—things my
son no longer recognizes, accustomed as he is to only sweet
potatoes and bananas.

The huge commercial market was unique in all the nine-
teen municipalities of Havana. Groups of informal vendors
offered "persecuted" products such as cheese and evapo-
rated milk. The meager assortment of what we receive from
the rationed market was also on sale. Many sold their subsidized rations to cover other needs, such as the electricity
bill or shoes for the children. We all benefited from this illegal exchange, except the State, because these transactions
occurred outside its control.

Now, in the new and orderly Four Roads Market, your
wallet is no longer in jeopardy, but there is no toothpaste
for ten Cuban pesos a tube nor detergent for twenty a tablet.
The merchandise that was offered by the sellers there cannot be found anywhere at the same prices, and the unruly
mess is no more. But the formula of discipline, constraint,
and control doesn't appear to please the disoriented shop-
pers, who continue to long for the market as it was, before
the police operation.

The hand that throws the sticks

As in a game of pick-up sticks, in which a fistful of thin sticks is dropped from above, so my colleagues and I have been scattered across the enormous tabletop of the globe. Those of us who studied, exchanged ideas, and worked on projects together now make up a network of University of Havana philology graduates all over the world.

Marlen, from Matanzas, lives on the other shore and studies for her doctorate. Nelson, who was the first to graduate, has been in the United States for almost six years already. I know that the poet José Félix used to sing with his guitar in the bars of Spain, and Walfrido—who excelled in semantics—is with his girlfriend in Madrid. Many of the students who graduated ahead of me, such as Sahily and Yamilé, make a living in the New York or Latin America. The list of emigrants matches, with few exceptions, the School of Arts and Letters' roster during the years I studied there.

The pick-up stick that is me has done its tumbling from one continent to another, but a crazy gravitational force finally returned it to its origin. Because of this, I don't resent those who fell away. For all of us, a variety of circumstances threw us from here to there. "The hand that threw the sticks" was, for some, economic necessity, the lack of prospects, or the simple impossibility of continuing to live under one roof with parents and grandparents. Others were driven into exile by the suffocating lack of freedoms, the desire to shout on a street corner even if nobody hears.

The loss of all these linguists, writers, and art critics has caused irreversible damage to Cuban culture. Needless to say, the mass escape of my classmates engenders no expressions of regret in cultural conferences, or in meet-ings of the Cuban Writers and Artists Union, much less in political forums. No hand seems willing to reunite all these "sticks," to provide these "philologists in flight" the chance to have their own homes, to fulfill their professional dreams, or to shout—freely—from any street corner.

Men's matters

In this Central Havana of *guapos*—tough guys—and brawls where I was born, I learned that there are certain lines a woman should never cross.* I have spent my life breaking the laughable rules of machismo, but today—and only to-day—I am going to take refuge in one of them, one of those that I dislike the most. It warns, "A woman needs a man to represent her and to go to bat for her when another man insults or slanders her."

Feeling attacked by someone with a power infinitely superior to mine, more than twice my age, and in addi-tion—as the neighbors of my childhood would have said—someone who is "macho-male-masculine," I have decided it will be my husband, the journalist Reinaldo Escobar, who will respond.

I refer to the damaging remarks that Fidel Castro made about me in the prologue of the book *Fidel, Bolivia and Something More.* Not even such a "great" attack convinces

---

*Please do not confuse a Cuban *guapo* with a handsome man or suitor. That might work in another Latin American country, but here in Cuba the word carries a different connotation, which someone might explain to you with a slap, or perhaps a stabbing.

me to abandon the premise of refusing to engage in a cycle of rejoinder and self-defense. I am sorry to say I remain focused on the theme called "Cuba."

Let's leave it up to Reinaldo and Fidel to do the fighting. I will continue in my "womanly" labor of weaving together, despite the chatter, the frayed tapestry of our civil society.

The *guapos* from my neighborhood will know that I learned something from them!

Obligatory shadows

Two years ago, social workers knocked at my door. They came as part of the overblown "Energy Revolution" campaign to change my incandescent light bulbs for energy-savers. I liked the warm yellow light from the living-room lamp, but a quick inspection by trained teenagers revealed a wasteful filament and I had to give it up. They gave me another bulb that projected a pale light and lasted three weeks. My eyes were grateful for the short life of the economy bulb because at night there was no way to distinguish details under its fading light.

To replace the broken one, I turned to the foreign-currency stores. But they were no longer selling the demonized conventional bulbs—the ones I have had in the nightstand my whole life. I resigned myself to buying the short-lived energy-saving bulb or the other kind—called "cold light"— that makes my living room look like an operating room. But for the last two months, even those are not available. There are no light bulbs of any kind in the stores of Havana.

The clerks jokingly tell me that the boat "hasn't come from China yet" and inform me that a little shop in the Cerro district rescued a few bulbs during a moment of "public disorder." In my ill-lit apartment the shadows are overtaking the light. If this continues, I'll have to improve my sense of touch or trip over the furniture.

What nobody knows—and I only write these secrets in a private diary like this one—is that I managed to hide, from the social workers, one specimen of the persecuted bulbs. It is round and wasteful and, with its yellow 40-watt light, has been with me for more than five years. It is not that it is a pleasure to waste electricity, but I need to believe that I can decide, at least, under which type of light I read, cook, or watch television.

I cling to the forbidden bulb as if it could illuminate not only my living room, but the stupidity of the retailers and the pig-headedness of the energy campaigners.

The Kingdom of adidas

Her Nike sneakers stick out their tongues at my fake leather sandals, while I calculate that her Italian sunglasses cost an entire month's wages. From her purse, purchased from Via Uno, she pulls out some Marlboros and offers me one, even though she knows I don't smoke. We go together to her house in Cerro, a crumbling old tenement occupied by seven families. I enter the living room and her impeccable shoes clash with the backless metal chair, the amorphous mattress covered by a gray sheet, and walls that haven't been painted since her grandfather died. She offers me coffee in a cup without a handle, but all I see is the gold ring on her index finger. "Yadira!" I rebuke her. "You dress with such opulence and you don't even have your own bathroom!" She smiles and I can see a small ruby embedded in her left eyetooth.

Leaving her house I can't help but notice the incongruent combination of ostentation and misery that adorns our streets. Amid the deteriorating doorways on Avenida Reina I see adidas, Kelme, and Wilson coming and going. My nose picks up the stench of an open sewer running across the sidewalk, as well as the unmistakable essence of Christian Dior. The lines outside the boutiques speak of the money coming in through remittances, illegal activities, and the diversion of resources from State enterprises, which sustains the fancies of these peacocks. No one wants to go without brand name clothing, be it fake or authentic.

I'm told that the adidas store, located on the corner of First and D in Vedado, has the highest sales per square foot of all their Latin America stores. They are even thinking of moving to a larger site to double their profits. Some of the products they sell will be bought by people who don't have their own home, or who have to juggle just to be able to eat each day. They prefer to wear their most "valuable" possessions on their bodies.

From behind the UV lenses of her sunglasses, draped in the cotton of a Point Zero garment, with her L'Oreal-scented hair, Yadira does not see the falling tiles in her kitchen nor the springs popping out of her mattress. To those who know her, she is a magnificent young woman dressed in the latest styles, and not the resident of a poor tenement where, each morning, she carries her own water into the tiny collective bathroom.

The turn of the "thirds"

The whole family is searching for papers that prove the Spanish origin of their maternal grandparents. They rummage through the archives, questioning those who were once neighbors of a cantankerous Asturian and her sweetheart from the Canary Islands who became her husband. They already have the birth certificates and baptism records for all the aunts and uncles, and they have managed to finagle Internet access to investigate Ellis Island databases. Before November they must have a family tree proving that they are the grandchildren of Spaniards, "third" generation in a line of descent that could guarantee them a new passport.

The Spanish Embassy in Havana is preparing for the tsunami of Cubans who can present proof of their Spanish ancestry, the descendants of those who once journeyed to this island in search of better lives. Many of these mid-twentieth-century immigrants went native, lost the accent and ended up Cuban. Now their grandchildren want to take the return trip, pushed by lack of opportunity and material hardships.

My neighbor Yampier is among the nearly three million Cubans interested in recovering their Spanish heritage. To acquaint himself he has started to read the biography of the Spanish royals, Juan Carlos and Sofia, to say "Madriz" and not "Madri" as we pronounce it here. He has become a fanatic follower of Barça, Barcelona's soccer team, and recites fragments from the thirteenth century epic poem *El Cantar del Mio Cid* better than many Spaniards. His gray passport, the one that says *República de Cuba,* viewed with wary eyes in all the airports of the world, is now put away in a drawer.

In a few years, when someone asks him about his origins, he will say something like, "Part of my childhood and youth was spent in Cuba, but really I'm Spanish." However, his grandmother, Asunción, and his grandfather, Francisco, remain at rest, as was their wish, in the *Cementerio de Colón* in the city of Havana.

A diploma and lot of confusion

The school year ended and already I see a danger to my bread ration. My son will be out of school for over two months and, in the excitement of the holiday, could eat the hinges off the doors. He cannot be satisfied with the floury specimen of 80 grams that is his daily bread ration, and he is sure to attack my or his dad's quota.

Meanwhile, I am preparing myself for the typical questions, "Mom, aren't we going to visit our family in Camagüey?" I try to explain to him that the line for the interprovincial bus is three days long and they are already selling tickets for the second half of July. Nor will it appease him to know that the price of taking one of the new Chinese articulated buses to the center of the Island is half the average worker's monthly salary.

But I will try to please him and cede my bread, sleep three days in the line for a ticket to Camagüey, and until then even rent a couple hours of PlayStation time from a neighbor. All this because he has finished seventh grade with good marks and deserves to be rewarded. Last Saturday, the end of the school year, he returned home with his diploma, and let out his war cry from the doorway, "I'm on vacation!"

The only thing is, I don't know if my son has graduated from the seventh grade or from the Communist Party "Ñico Lopez" School. The confusion began when I saw the diploma, which is not at all clear on the subject.

Something to escape

She can withstand a double workday, one as a secretary and the other as a mother and a homemaker, thanks to a few Valium hidden in her handbag. No doctor prescribed the drug; instead she herself found her path to peace by trying different medications. Only under the small pills' influence—an ever greater dosage—can she tolerate the Party meetings, the food lines, and the difficulty of feeding her family.

At first she bought pills from a neighbor who took them from a pharmaceutical warehouse. She experimented with Librium and Elavil and was able to sleep at night, to smile when the bus ran half an hour late. After a raid on the black market, her supplier went to jail, and she lacked the sedatives that she needed. A new seller soon appeared, with much higher prices.

Nobody in the family wants to admit that mom lives in the clouds, with a strangely satisfied face, even while dealing with problems and shortages. Her evasion is quieter than her husband's drunken shuffle as he returns home, almost falling down. Both of them have chosen their escape, each using what they have at hand; he, alcohol distilled at the hospital by a skilled hand, and she, a pill that makes her forget about her own life.

Nor can the children adapt themselves to this reality. They'd rather nurture dreams of escape, although in a more tangible way. They keep a half-assembled motor underneath the bed, and this August they'll purr across the Florida Straits. Their mother won't worry about them. Double the Valium dosage, and she'll avoid torturing herself with thoughts of sharks, sunstroke, and the separation from her children that awaits her.

Cyber-mutilated

Working in cyberspace and developing our own projects on the Internet raises all the issues of citizenship that are too big for Cubans to handle. We haven't been able to become citizens of the real world, so we find it difficult to act like citizens in the virtual world. And there are no shortcuts. We can't simply skip over interim stages as we did with videocassettes (which were never sold in the "peso stores"anyway), tape recorders, and the big floppy disks.[6] Instead we must first educate ourselves in civics right here in real life.

Let's see if I can understand the twisted logic of Cuban cyberspace. "It is not possible for a Cuban citizen to establish her own web domain and house it on a server in Cuba;

but it is illegal for her to establish a web domain hosted on a server in another country." "Cuba's 'official' bloggers reflect the only true reality. We, the alternative bloggers, therefore, are puppets of some foreign power." "The Internet is the terrain where the so-called 'Battle of Ideas' is fought. The one principle that defines this battle is: Intolerance."[7] In short, in addition to the mutilation of our society, we enter cyberspace—our virtual society—similarly maimed.

At this point, we see the same behavior on the Internet that we see on our streets. When placed in front of cameras and microphones, people's first reaction is to show enthusiasm and ideological fidelity, but their behavior is pure froth. That is why, on the Internet, we call ourselves folklorists and environmentalists. It's OK to post employment ads and classified ads, or to distribute free music online, but one needs to be careful about expressing opinions. On the World Wide Web we must hide behind the same masks we wear in our daily lives. Having cyber-rights will have to wait for the day when we can at last begin to become full citizens.

Carnivals

The Havana Malecón is getting ready for Carnival.[8] On the Piragua, tents are set up for restaurants serving international food and colorful kiosks are everywhere. [9] The metal structures used for reviewing stands are ready, while groups practice the choreography they will show off beginning Friday, August 1.

Because the dates for our popular celebrations

constantly change, we are never sure when carnivals start. Their announcement surprises us, and we aren't even very disappointed when they are suspended. I remember the summer of 2006, when we were allowed only painted floats because Havana's conga drums didn't fit with the somber mood of Fidel Castro's illness.

Luckily, this year, the bands might play. It is a schizo-phrenic carnival: Most of the products are sold for convert-ible pesos, with a small portion of the pleasures set aside for those who have only Cuban pesos. Due to violence and poverty, carnival is no longer a place for the whole family. But even so, it is a time to shrug off the slogans, the short-ages, and the frustrated expectations. Dancing is a magnifi-cent way of forgetting.

So we will have a festival along the same perimeter of coast where, fourteen years ago, *Habaneros* demonstrated their discontent in a social uprising we called the *Malecon-azo*.[10] We will drink along the same wall that felt the weight of makeshift rafts heading north. We will enjoy salsa and reggaeton on the same oceanfront boulevard where no "of-ficial" demonstrators have chanted slogans and waved little flags for months. To this Malecón, which has witnessed our shouts, our departures, and our feigned sentiments, we will go, for a few days, to amuse ourselves.

Two years

He drank brandy and watched the vultures fly, as they did every day, around the Plaza of the Revolution. It was a Tuesday, the first of August, 2006, and he was looking over the balcony for the changes that would come. The night before, they had read a proclamation on television saying the Maximum Leader was temporarily delegating his powers. He met with friends and they spent the early morning hours talking about the future, while the streets remained strangely empty.

During the first weeks after the announcement, he paid close attention to the news and bought some canned food so he wouldn't have to go outside. He dusted off his Chinese radio, which, from one corner of the bathroom, could pick up shortwave radio broadcasts. In the meantime, he avoided changing the euros his mother had sent him and stocked up on candles and batteries.

After six months, he stopped looking out the window, reading between the lines of the newspaper, and tape-recording everything that seemed to be a testament to "the final days." He met again with his friends, but this time they talked about the 1980s, high school, and the Special Period.

Two years later, on July 31, sitting with his back to the city, he received a postcard from his ex-girlfriend in Jerusalem. It had been some weeks since he'd watched the news or tuned in to the illegal radio stations. Late one night he told us that his mother had asked him to come to Italy to live with her. As not a single whiff of transformation could be smelled from his terrace, he said yes.

Coexistence and its dangers

I heard screaming and realized that for a couple of weeks she had been wearing dark glasses so no one could see the bruises. Her husband is a Party militant, and nobody in the neighborhood criticizes his testosterone-fueled excesses. It is part of a pattern of domestic violence, ignored by the media, but a reality of everyday life. The victims feel doubly battered. Because added to the slap and the scream is the silence of those who don't want to believe, let alone make it public, that all is not harmony and respect behind the doors of Cuban homes.

Forced cohabitation due to lack of housing leaves many women and children subject to humiliation and beatings. We don't hear their testimony because, institutionally, domestic violence is barely recognized on this "idyllic island." With the statistics that would prove its frequency unreported, it is very difficult to influence public opinion or to bring it to bear to reject these attacks.

How can a woman, who flees home to avoid her husband's fists, know how to find a shelter if not through the media? How can she know about her right to bring her attacker to court if not from the TV and newspapers? How can we condemn the abusers when we barely acknowledge their victims? We watch them putting up with it, hiding the punches under rouge, and eyeing us to see if we acknowledge what the institutions and the media won't.

To go up and down

More than twenty years of repairing the Soviet elevator and climbing up and down stairs are nearing an end. Two brand-new Russian elevators have just been delivered to my building to replace the obsolete socialist technology.

We had to wait until the ancient machinery was actually a "danger to life." The military buildings nearby take priority in the replacement of elevators. And we had to wait for Cuban-Russian relations to once again flourish.

I'm happy because my husband Reinaldo won't have to spend so much time repairing the prehistoric elevator. Thanks to those who, twenty years ago, expelled him from his profession, the residents of our one hundred and forty-four apartments have benefited from his skills as a journalist-turned-elevator-mechanic. One who, living on the fourteenth floor, had has a great interest in seeing the elevator repaired. Only through our persistence has it been possible to extend the life of something that should have been replaced years ago. The solutions found by citizens are often touted as "achievements of the system," when in reality they are desperate struggles for survival.

After a decade of cannibalizing one of the elevators for parts to keep the other running, we are looking forward to the replacements. The installation will last about four months, during which time I will burn many calories on the two hundred and thirty-two steps separating me from the street. However, the intense exercise doesn't scare me; I have climbed these fourteen floors with my bike on my shoulder, and while carrying a mattress and, many, many times, with my son in my arms. Now I'll do it with the incentive that soon we'll have two new elevators. They won't be Soviet, but rather—and here it is worth pointing out the difference—simply "Russian."

Uterus on strike

I was going to call her Gea and she would have relieved Teo
of being an only child. For her, I would have once again pu-
reed malanga, boiled bottles at night, and washed loads of
diapers. But thinking better of it, Gea remained the unmet
desire for a second child. I looked ahead twenty years—and
imagined today's same housing problems with two married
children who would bring their spouses to live with us. At
first, with three marriages under one roof, we would try to
maintain harmony, but conflicts would inevitably arise.

Our house, like so many, would have several generations
living together, with suppressed battles taking place every
day: The refrigerator divided into multiple zones; couples
making love quietly because of the nearness of the other
beds; the grandchildren sharing their grandparents' bed-
room with their grandparents—in this case my husband's
and mine—making them feel like they are already a nui-
sance for the youngsters. The children would spend a good
part of the day in the corridor or on the street, because of
the little space at home. Soon they would be teenagers and
look for partners themselves, new potential occupants for
a house already bursting at the seams.

Before hurricanes Gustav and Ike, my generation and
my son Teo's had to wait forty years or more to have a house.
Now the period has surpassed the span of a human life. Together with the roofing tiles and the windows taken by the
winds, the hurricanes sent flying so many people's dreams
of having their own roof. Where there are no resources to
replace what the victims lost, how long will it be for those
who had nothing to begin with?

Without sentimentality, Gea has vanished totally from my life. I know that we have no space for her.

Which came first?

Prices are rising sharply in the informal market. An egg now costs four Cuban pesos, one-third the average wage for a day's labor. But it's not the buyers who are the hardest-hit; for those who illegally sell this product, a conviction can lead to two years in prison. This measure is meant to eliminate gouging after the destruction of the poultry farms caused by hurricanes Gustav and Ike. Reckless black-market traders are processed in summary trials as a lesson to all who illegally trade in food, construction materials or medicines. Our police—long trained in detecting beef, cheese, shrimp, and powdered milk—now search out eggs as well.

As a result of these new raids, certain products that were sold door-to-door have disappeared. These days, chanting "Eeee-eeeggs" may be more dangerous than chanting anti-government slogans. OK, let's not exaggerate. Opinion is always punished more heavily. But the new crackdown against the informal market has helped resolve the age-old riddle, "Which came first?" We now know it was the egg. They arrested those who sold homemade sweets, later they prosecuted those who protested the fuel price hike, and finally, they punished those who reported on the scarcity of products in the markets. Who knows, by the time it's the turn of those who traffic in chicken, the prison term may exceed the length of a human life!

The ghost of *Pravda*

The most important stories in the newspaper do not come with headlines that betray their contents. Under the vague headlines "Informing the Population," "Letter from the Ministry of the Interior," or "Declaration of the State Council," we learn about the most significant events. This Monday, September 29, *Granma* trumpeted in huge letters, "Information for Our People." The elderly—who buy the papers to resell to supplement their pensions—quickly bought up all the newspapers and raised the price to two Cuban pesos for today's copy of the official organ of the Cuban Communist Party.

"*Granma* is authorized to report," the newspaper announced, just as the Soviet *Pravda* used to do. The expression made me think about how much news they are ordered not to report in our largest circulation daily, and with what discipline they comply. But I shook off the Stalinist reminders and continued reading. After a few paragraphs it was clear that it is not only the paper's layout that recalls the worst of the Soviet press, but the tone and the threats as well. Warning that "any attempt to violate the law or the rules of social coexistence will be met with a swift and forceful response," the editorial threatens speculators, profiteers, and sellers in the informal market, letting them know that punishment awaits them.

I was especially confused by a paragraph pointing out: "Punishment will invariably be enforced in the face of such actions, and against all signs of privilege, corruption or theft..." How could the General Prosecutor of the Republic cope with the huge number of privileges proliferating on this Island, granted to the ideologically loyal? Will the punished excesses include the beach house where the lieutenant colonel vacations with his family? The shopping bag with chicken and detergent given to the censor for filtering Web pages? The access to preferential prices enjoyed by the whistle-blowers and the "vultures" of State Security? These are the privileges I see around me, but I don't think that *Granma* has launched a crusade against them. To do so would be an act of self-cannibalism.

The title of this article should be "It threatens Our People," because we are all included in the harsh words directed at criminals. Because who in this country doesn't cross the line of illegality to buy something? What citizen doesn't depend on the black market? How many families survive by diverting resources from their State jobs to offset the indignity of their salaries? Which are the systems of distribution that aren't plagued by corruption, despicable but tolerated by the State because it is one of the safety valves that prevents a social explosion?

The ghost of *Pravda* is not the only ghost I saw while reading this article. I also saw that of radicalization, the iron fist, and the State of Emergency—a constant state of battle with which our leaders feel so comfortable.

The longest war

On Thursday, a movie about the Cuban war in Angola was released across the island. Outside the movie theaters, couples changed course and headed someplace dark instead. The Cuban campaign in Africa holds little interest for them.

The film suffers from a couple of decades' delay and tackles a story which is still partly classified. *Kangamba* would have generated long lines and impassioned comment at the end of the '80s, but at this point very few want to remember what happened.

Angola was the longest war in Cuban history—fifteen years of fighting in another land, killing or being killed by people who barely knew where this Island is. That was when the Kremlin was casting its long shadow over Cuba. We depended on them so heavily that our leaders did not hesitate to join in their campaign against UNITA. Geopolitics devises these difficult tests for the small countries that orbit great empires.

During that decade-and-a-half-long conflict, no Cuban mothers staged protests against sending their sons to the front. No one in the media dared to ask what we all whispered: "What are we doing in Angola?" Nor was there a peace movement with white doves in front of each recruiting station. We were more docile as citizens than we are today, and they took us to die and to kill without our knowing why.

Today, we are informed about every loss suffered by the American army in Iraq, but I remember the secrecy surrounding how many Cuban soldiers died during the Angolan War. We knew that a neighbor had lost a son, or that a colleague had returned without a leg, but the press only trumpeted victory. The dead were mourned by their families in private—families who did not understand why their children were fighting on the other side of the Atlantic. The niches in the cemetery remained, the framed photos in the family rooms, the flowers at every anniversary, and the long speeches from those who had seen the war from afar, but nobody knew how to respond with clarity to the question, "What are Cubans doing in Angola?"

Bouillon cubes

I argued with a lady in line for malanga root. She wanted to let her two friends cut in, and I figured that if they did I wouldn't get my ten pounds of food, rationed now since the hurricanes. In the end I let the two old ladies cut the line and didn't even insult them when the clerk announced, "It's closed, there's no more!" It depresses me to get into a fight over food, which is probably why I'm so skinny. In high school, I never had the claws to grab for a better share and it always went to the strongest. When I see myself reduced to fighting for food, I feel bad and prefer to come home with an empty shopping bag.

Of course my family doesn't thank me for my excessive pacifism. To console them, I bought a few boxes of bouillon cubes, which is now the most common staple for the majority of the people in this city. When some confused tourist asks me what a typical Cuban dish is, I answer that I don't remember, but I know the most common everyday recipes. And I list them: "Rice with a beef bouillon cube," "rice with a hot dog," "rice with a bacon bouillon cube," or the delicacy of "rice with a chicken-and-tomato bouillon cube." This last one has a color between pink and orange that is most amusing.

If we're constantly being fed predigested news on the

television, canned speeches past their expiration date, little cubes of patience and waiting, smidgens of getting by day-to-day, why shouldn't our plates reflect these same bitter flavors? So, I resign myself and buy the happy placebo that will make me believe that my rice contains a tasty rib or a piece of chicken. After the most "complicated" preparation, I put the steaming dish on the table. My son, smelling the odor, asks me reproachfully, "Why didn't you fight harder in the line for malanga?"

Terminations

"Twenty-three-years-old and four abortions," she's telling everyone who wants to hear. On her slim figure, maternity would wreak havoc, she tells me, while adjusting her short skirt around her hips. For many years abortion was the most common method of birth control for thousands of Cuban women. In the eighties, condoms were an illusion, and when they finally became available, men refused to use them.

I met this slender young woman from Villa Clara on a Chinese-made bus bound for that province. In the first hour of conversation she told me all the details of her truncated pregnancies. "It doesn't hurt much," she told me, while winking at the driver who was looking at her legs in the rearview mirror. In her almost forty-minute lecture, she wanted to explain her reasons, although I knew them already from others. That she lives with her parents and shares a room with her sister; that of the men she's been intimate with, some are married or don't want to have

children; that she wants to leave the country and it's harder
with a baby… she ended by making clear, "I have a friend
in the gynecological hospital and she always fixes it for me."

I was rattled by her illusion that she can leave all her
problems—housing, love or immigration—in the operating room, and I pointed out that they are no longer doing
abortions in hospitals. The press hasn't written about it.
Just as no one has talked about the high number of dila-
tion-and-curettages that were practiced until very recently.
But for the last few months an internal directive has limited the number of terminations of pregnancy. The reason
is that the birth rate is falling, and they want to try to increase it, even if it means forcing women to give birth. She
bit her lip in disbelief and declared with some cheek, "Don't
worry yourself, I took a nice gift to the doctor and left
with a brand-new womb." The bus hit a rut and I noticed
that the driver was still entranced with her thighs. I was
afraid we were going to crash and we'd end up like another
aborted trip.

Something could begin this Tuesday

The streets are not the same, nor are the neighbors who
usually gossip in the lines at the markets; today they speak
of universal themes. They raise their eyebrows and point
towards the north, while they make predictions about who
will be elected at the polls in the US I don't remember having lived through such commotion during Cuban presiden-
tial elections. The cobbler in my building took a stand for
one candidate and the old woman who sells flowers has

been wearing an Obama T-shirt. Our boring history of two presidents in fifty years has exacerbated this curiosity over foreign elections. But we also know that the decision of US voters will reverberate in Cuba and not so metaphorically as the flutter of a butterfly's wings in the Amazon.

The remittances that allow thousands of Cuban families to get to the end of the month come primarily from the US, where a great portion of this Island now lives, and where the insults—"worms," traitors," and "mafiosi"—have not managed to sever our emotional and family ties. Our leaders would lose all effectiveness without the United States in the role of enemy. Never has the destiny of Cuba been so clearly separated, and yet so dependent, on what happens ninety miles away. So, we are all waiting to see who will win this Tuesday, November 4.

Those whose children can only come visit every three years are confident that the Democratic candidate will be more flexible in allowing visits to the Island. Others are betting that the heavy hand of the Republicans will manage to force the openings we have expected for decades. In the face of the "uncertain prognosis" inside our own country, some say today's results will either launch or derail the cart of reform in Cuba.

I would prefer that we drive ourselves, but very few want to exchange forecasting for the hard work of making things happen. As I write this post, the capricious vehicle of change seems to be stuck in a rut on the side of the road. I have my doubts about whether what happens Tuesday will get it moving.

Hospitals: You bring everything?

A bucket in one hand, a pillow under my arm, and an electric fan balanced on my hip, I enter the door of the oncology hospital. The backpack over my shoulder blocks the custodian from seeing my face. It's of little importance, because the man is used to the fact that patients' families must bring everything, so my baroque structure of fans, bucket, and pillowcase doesn't surprise him. He doesn't know it yet, but somewhere in a bag hanging off me I've brought him an omelet sandwich so he'll let me stay after visiting hours.

I come into the room and Mónica is holding her mother's hand. Her mother's face is more and more haggard. She has cancer of the esophagus and there is little that can be done, although the woman still doesn't know that. I've never understood doctors' refusals to inform patients of how little time is left before the end. But I respect the decision of the family, although I don't join in the lie that she will soon be well. The room has a thin light and the air smells of pain.

I begin to unpack what I've brought. I take out the little sack of detergent and the aromatic with which I'll clean the bathroom; its "aroma" floods everything. With the bucket we can bathe her mother, because the water faucet doesn't work. For the heavy scrubbing I brought a pair of yellow gloves, frightened of the germs that spread in a hospital. Mónica tells me to continue unpacking and I extract a package of food and a puree especially for the sick. The pillow has been a wonder and a set of clean sheets manages to cover the mattress, stained with successive effluvia.

The most welcome item is the fan, which I connect to two peeled wires hanging from the wall.

Continuing, I come to the little bag of medical supplies. I have obtained some needles appropriate for the IV, because the one in her arm is very thick and causes pain. I also bought some gauze and cotton on the black market. The most difficult—which cost me days and an incredible series of swaps—is suture thread for the surgery they will do tomorrow. I also brought a box of disposable syringes since she yells to high heaven when the nurse approaches her with a glass one. To distract her, I've come loaded with a radio, and a nearby patient has brought a television. My friend and her mom can watch the soap operas, while I look for the doctor and give him a gift sent by the sick woman's husband.

When bedtime comes, a cockroach crosses the wall near the bed and I remember that I also brought some insect spray. In the backpack I still have some medicines and a little gift for the girl in the lab. I have money in my pocket, because ambulances are for the most critical cases and when they send her home, terminally ill, we will need to take a Panataxi.

In the next bed is an old woman, who eats the watery soup she's given by the hospital staff. Around her bed there's no bag brought by her family and she doesn't have a pillow for her head. I position the fan so that she will also get the cool air, and we talk about the arrival of another hurricane. Without her realizing it I knock on the wood of the doorframe, whether to expel the fear of disease or in horror at the conditions in the hospital, I really don't know.

A woman passes by shouting that she has bread and ham for sale for the visitors and I lock myself in the bathroom, which smells like jasmine after my cleaning.

The reprimands of Wednesday

At nine in the morning, a bored official looks at the citation Reinaldo and I present at the door of the Twenty-first and C police station. We are left waiting on one of the benches for about forty minutes, and we take the opportunity to discuss all those things we never get to in the vertigo of daily life. At 9:45 they take my husband, first asking if he has a cell phone. Ten minutes later, they return and take me to the second floor.

The meeting is brief and the tone energetic. There are three of us in the office; the one who raises his voice is introduced as Agent Roque. To my side another, younger one, watches me, he says his name is Camilo. Both tell me they are from the Interior Ministry. They are not interested in listening; there is a written script on the table, and nothing I do will distract them. They are intimidation professionals.

The topic is as I expected. We are nearing the date for the blogger meeting we have been organizing for half a year, with neither secrecy nor publicity; they announce that we must cancel it. Half an hour later, now far from the uniforms and the photos of leaders on the walls, we reconstruct an approximation of their words:

> We want to warn you that you have transgressed all limits of tolerance with your rapprochement and contact with

counterrevolutionary elements. This totally disqualifies you
for dialog with the Cuban authorities.

The activities planned for the coming days cannot be
carried out.

We, for our part, will take all measures, file the relevant
reports, and take the necessary actions. This activity, at this
moment in the life of the Nation, recuperating from two hur-
ricanes, will not be allowed.

Roque stopped talking—nearly shouting—and I asked
if he would give me all this in writing. Being a blogger who
displays her name and her face has made me believe that
everyone is willing to attach their identity to what they say.
The man lost the rhythm of his script—he didn't expect my
librarian's mania for saving and sorting papers. He stopped
reading what had been written and shouted at me, even
louder, "We are not obliged to give you anything!"

Before he sent me off with a "Get out of here, citizen," I
managed to say to him that he won't sign what he had just
told me because he doesn't have the courage to do it. The
word "cowards" comes out almost as a guffaw. At the bottom of the stairs I hear the noise of the chairs pushed back
into place. Wednesday has ended early.

Brief encounter with Mariela Castro

Yesterday, December 11, I went to a conference on sexuality
at the Museum of Fine Arts. For the last two weeks, a series on erotic art has been accompanied by films and talks.
Just this Tuesday there was a chance to hear about the

incorporation of transsexuals into society and the preju-
dices that still exist against them. So on the way to Alamar—
where the Festival of Poetry Without End is underway—I
dropped into the amphitheater in the old Asturian Center.

After the conference, I had the chance to ask Mariela
Castro a question that torments me every time I hear about
tolerance for sexual preference. I still don't understand that
we accept the right of another to choose with whom they
make love, yet we continue in this ideological monogamy
they have imposed. If concepts such as "sick" have now
been banished from the study of homosexuality, why does
the adjective "counterrevolutionary" continue to be applied
to those who think differently? For me, to call someone
who doesn't conform in their sexuality a "faggot" is no different from calling someone who doesn't conform in their
ideology a "worm."

As today is the day that these rights should be at the
center of everyone's attention, I want to show a short video
of my brief encounter with Mariela. The audio is poor and
so I have transcribed the dialog for those who are unable to
hear everything.

MARIELA: *Including treatment for transgender people is something that's called for in the law. We don't ask for more.*

YOANI: *I'd like to ask if this entire campaign for society to accept sexual preference could, at some point, move to other areas? Will it also fight for tolerance of other differences, other
points of view and political and ideological preference? Will we
also "come out of the closet" in these areas?*

MARIELA: *I don't know because I don't work in that area. The ideological and political field is outside my responsibility. I think I am doing the best I can given my ability.*

Gallita / "cocky hen"

A curious year-end in which surprises accumulate, Christmas trees return, and sexologists start to use the language of the *machistas*—the sexists. Mariela Castro has called me a *gallita*—a female cock. In her language as a specialist in gender and sexuality, the word has homophobic connotations. Perhaps because I am ignorant of the language of her specialty, I fail to understand what she wants to tell me by saddling me with a masculine role in a feminine noun; with regards to grammar, I can boast about knowing a thing or two. Does she believe that I do the work of a man because I demand my rights and respect for political preferences? I don't see the feathers on my tail, but if to be a delicate hen I must accept that a group of septuagenarians—all men—decide every aspect of my life, then I'm inclined to transvestism and will cock-a-doodle-doo like the most testosterone-filled rooster in the barnyard.

In his flowery apron, my husband Reinaldo laughs and confirms that yes, I'm a "cocky hen" with sharpened spurs. I agree with the prestigious specialist that I am "insignificant," an anonymous hen who, with her *cheep cheep*, has managed to inconvenience the fine fighting cocks. The ones with so little experience in debate that at the slightest disagreement they jump up and let feathers fly, lashing out on all sides. They get upset and end up sticking out their

tongues so we can see—inside—the ugly entrails of intolerance, which lately they work so hard to hide.

Christmas Day

Today could be the third of June or the ninth of September,
because there are hardly any signs that it is Christmas. Few,
very few, offer holiday greetings in the street. Compared
to December 25 of last year, this is a lifeless day with fewer
expectations for the future. More than twelve months
have passed since we predicted—in the privacy of family
and friends—anticipated reforms, which turned out to be
nothing more than a mobile phone or a room in a hotel that
we can't afford.

Today the rooster will crow for a people whose actions
are reduced to the deliberately complacent verb: to wait.*
Meanwhile, my address book fills with the phone numbers
of friends who have emigrated, and our president jumps
like a caged cat when they speak to him of imprisoned dissidents. What little progress we've made in 2008! What a
ridiculous marching in place we've managed, right up to
December.

---

*Tradition has it that the only time the rooster crowed at midnight
was the night of Jesus' birth.

2009

Celebration and ground beef

To mark the country's fifty year anniversary of January 1, we were allowed to buy a half-pound of ground beef through the ration system. With the humor that often saves us from going crazy, this unexpected delicacy was dubbed "Chavez's hamburger," referring to the obvious economic shoring-up coming from Venezuela.

For its fiftieth anniversary the grand socialist revolution should aspire to more ambitious things—but there is not much to give. Although it seems frivolous, for many Cubans getting that beef was the most significant event of recent times. Its flavor will be what we remember of a gray December and an equally haggard January, with not so much as the vague promise of improvement or reform.

A Step Forward

Andy is one of those who doesn't wait. He had a mobile phone when they were only for foreigners, bought an apartment through an obsolete housing law, and, since 2008, has been selling toasters that *Granma* announced wouldn't be available until 2010. He goes to the large stores that sell in convertible pesos and offers his merchandise, which is diverted from state warehouses. He's a man of his time and yet a man of the future, too—the complete product of a long era of illegalities.

He rents movies and soap operas copied from a satellite dish that he hides in a water tank. His clients always ask for something with sex, a lot of action, and little politics. He satisfies them. Whatever is banned is the direct source of his earnings. And, given that there is so much one can't do, he is a king in the country of the forbidden. This young man, not yet forty, sniffs out any restrictions that create a niche market. His long experience in subterfuges has taught him that respecting the penal code and survival are contradictory actions. So, when criticized for being an illegal vendor, he says he only provides what the State doesn't or what it sells at prohibitive prices.

His pocket dictates his ethics, and he has scammed some who trusted him too much. Nothing keeps him from sleeping peacefully at night because he knows that among his victims are those who also cheat others. His generation grew up seeing their parents steal from the State and were taught the ruthless code of taking everything within reach. Maybe one day they'll nab him and put him behind bars. But it won't change anything. In this town there are many Andys.

Lady, I love you

I am waiting on a bench in Central Park for some friends who are already half an hour late. It's been a hard day and I have little desire to speak with anyone. A boy, he can't be more than twenty, sits down next to me. He speaks English badly but asks me where I'm from and if I understand Spanish. My first impulse is to tell him to beat it, I'm not looking for *jineteros* hunting for tourists, but I let him go on with his seduction.[11]

I don't know if it's the pale skin I inherited from my Spanish grandparents, but my passport is just as blue and Cuban as his. If he didn't think I was a foreigner, he'd never come near me. I am not a good match—obviously he can see that—but he calculates that even if I look like a poor stranger, at least I could get him a visa to emigrate.

Encouraged by my silence, he says in English, "Lady, I love you," and after such a declaration of love I can't contain my laughter. I tell him in my best Central Havana slang, "Don't waste your bullets on me, I'm *cubiche*."[12] He jumps like he's been stung by red ants and starts insulting me. I can still hear him shouting, "This skinny thing looks like a foreigner but she's local and worth less than the national currency." My day has suddenly changed and I begin to laugh, alone on the bench, a few meters from the marble statue of José Martí.

A rematch comes quickly for the frustrated Casanova. A Nordic woman in shorts walks by and he repeats to her the same refrain he tried on me. She smiles and seems dazzled by his youth and his braids, which end in colored beads. I watch them leave together, while the lively youth declares his love in a language in which he barely knows a dozen words.

Come and live it

Inspired by one of the many tourist advertisements, an idea has occurred to me to attract visitors to the Island. It is not a nature tour or an historic tour of the country's plazas and monuments. "Come stay '*a lo cubano*,' like a Cuban," could be the campaign's slogan. That would be sure to lack interest for its target audience. "Come and live it!" it would say on the cover of the ration book, given out at the beginning of the adventure.

Accommodations would not look like the luxurious rooms in the hotels in Varadero or Cayo Coco. Our tour operators would suggest dingy rooms in Central Havana, tenements in Buena Vista, and a crowded shelter for hurricane victims. The tourists who buy this package wouldn't use convertible currency. Their budget allowance for a two-week stay would be half the average monthly wage, three hundred Cuban pesos. Thus, they could not ride in foreign-currency taxis or drive rental cars. Use of public transport would be a must.

Restaurants would be forbidden for those who opt for this excursion, but they would receive eighty grams of bread each day. Maybe they'd have the good fortune to enjoy half a pound of fish before they left on their return flights. To travel around the island they would have the option—instead of spending three days in line for a ticket—to buy a seat after only one day in line. They would be prohibited from sailing or renting a surfboard so that they wouldn't end their stay ninety miles away rather than in our Caribbean "paradise."

At the end of their visit, these adventurous tourists

would get the diploma: "Connoisseurs of Cuban Reality." But they would have to return several times to be properly "adapted" to our everyday absurdity. They will leave thinner, sadder, and with an obsession with food, which they will satisfy in their home supermarkets. And above all they will have a tremendous allergy to tourism ads. The golden advertisements of *mulatas*, rum, music, and dancing will not hide the collapsing buildings, frustration, and inertia of the Cuba they have known and lived.

We the people

Speeches put me to sleep, and a leader at a podium is the height of tedium to me. I associate microphones with calls for intransigence, and the praised oratory of some seems like screams meant to deafen the "enemy." At public events I usually manage to slip away, and I prefer the buzzing of a fly to the promises of a politician. I have heard so many seemingly endless harangues that I'm not the best person to endure a new lecture.

From the podiums, I have heard predictions of invasions that never come, economic plans that are never met, and even phrases as crude as, "Let the scum that leaves, go!" All of which is why I was so confused by the serene statement delivered today, January 20, by Barack Obama, with his carefully constructed arguments and invocations to harmony.

On reading his speech—I don't have an illegal satellite dish to watch it on TV—it seemed to me that he banished all rhetoric to the twentieth century. In the twenty-first century we have started to say good-bye to the convulsed eloquence that no longer moves us. I only hope that it will be "We, the People" who will write the speeches in the future.

Victim? No. Responsible.

I could spend the day frightened, hiding from the men stationed below. I could write about the personal price of this blog, complete with testimonies from those who have been "warned" that I am a dangerous person. My every article could be a long complaint or an accusing finger, looking outside myself to find fault. But as it happens, I feel myself not a victim, but the one responsible.

I know I have been silent, I have allowed a few to govern my island as though they were running a private hacienda. I accepted that others would make decisions that touch us all, while I hid behind being too young, too fragile. I am responsible for having donned my mask, for having used my son and my family as reasons not to dare. I applauded them— like almost everyone else—and then left my country when I was fed up. I told myself it's much easier to forget than to try to change anything. I let them mark my life with rancor and suspicion. I tolerated their infecting me with paranoia. In my teens, a raft in the middle of the ocean was my most frequently nurtured desire.

However, as I do not feel like a victim, I raise my skirt a little, and show my legs to the two men who now follow me everywhere. There is nothing more paralyzing than the sight of a woman's calf flashing in the sun in the middle of the street. I am not a martyr. I don't forget to smile. Laughter is like hard stones in the teeth of authoritarians. I get on with my life with only one regret: that everything I live today is the product of my earlier silence, the direct result of my former passivity.

Lokomotiv

He started with a pick and shovel, planting heavy crossbeams that support the train lines. His father had also been a railroad worker, and an uncle even drove freightcars loaded with cane up to the sugar refinery. I was very young and already his life was connected to the locomotive, with its line of loud, packed cars. After years of work, he finally had the controls in his hands, driving the metal serpent through the Cuban countryside. My father became an engineer, fulfilling a long family lineage, joined to the railroad for decades.

More than once he let me drive along a quiet stretch, while he supervised and showed me how to sound the horn. "We had trains here before Spain," my paternal grandfather would say whenever anyone asked about his work. So I grew up smelling the metal of brakes when they screeched to a stop and pulling my toy train through a countryside of plastic trees and miniature cows.

The collapse of socialism in Europe derailed the family profession. Many engines were sidelined for lack of parts. Trips were more infrequent and delays habitual. Leaving Havana for Santiago could be delayed twenty hours or three days. In some small towns, traincars were attacked

by needy peasants who would steal some of the goods. The
station's loudspeakers would repeat, "The departure of the
train to [...] has been cancelled." My father was left without
a job, while his colleagues began making a living through a
variety of illegal work.

The railroad in Cuba has never recovered. Aging rail
lines and long lines to buy tickets have given it a terrible
reputation. "At the rate we're going, we'll stop having rail-
roads before Spain..." my father says sarcastically. His gaze
is not on the wheel he's disassembling—in his new profession as bicycle repairman—but on the mass of iron that he
once drove along this long and narrow Island.

Ortega y Gasset, meet Cachita

We've been in Santiago de Cuba since Friday. My mother
asked me to bring stones from the Sanctuary of Cobre,and
my sister, like in the refrain from the traditional song, is
hoping for a "little Virgin of Charity."[13] However, we have
come for something more: To spread the virus called "The
Blogger Journey"to this province, where there is less access to the Internet than in Havana but the same need to
express opinions.[14]

The trip leaves me with a mix of impressions. I came
with the idea of finding a dancing and outgoing people, but
I go without having seen a single smile. The plaza where
Raúl Castro spoke of continuity a month ago is now full of
people hunting for tourists, and beggars who ask for money
for food. I walked streets filled with shops that trade only in
convertible pesos, and up steep streets with houses on the

verge of collapse. "Save water, we can only fill the tank once every two weeks," was the welcoming phrase from the kind family who put us up.

Today, Sunday morning, we had an interesting meeting. Young people filled with discontent and desire for change came to hear us talk about the Cuban blogosphere. Shy at first, soon many asked questions about the multifaceted, flexible tool that is a blog. Now we'll see if they join our *Voces Cubanas*—Cuban Voices—project.[15]

I went to the sanctuary of the Virgin of Charity of Cobre, an island within the Island, where offerings for the freedom of political prisoners and the insignias of the Rebel Army coexist in the same glass case. There, I left my Ortega y Gasset prize for journalism, the best place it could possibly be. Fortunately, the long arm of the censor does not enter her temple. Around Cachita still stretches one of the few strongholds of plurality that exist on this green crocodile of a country.

Fear of the end

Among my most intense impressions of Santiago de Cuba was of not being able to enjoy the same services as the foreign tourists there.

In the modern offices of the telecommunications company ETECSA, you can send a fax or connect to the Internet. But only if you can prove you weren't born in Cuba. I know this because staffers were staring at my clothes trying to determine if I were a foreigner or a national. As I am skilled in the art of slipping through cracks, I spoke a ridiculous hodgepodge of English and German and they sold me a card to access the Internet.

From there I sent last Sunday's post and watched while they refused Internet service to several Cubans who entered. Offering no explanation, just a simple "access is for tourists only," they prevented my fellow citizens from using idle computers. One man, particularly upset, protested. He said something like, "this is a lack of respect," and I, not able to continue faking that I was German, made a small correction: "This is another lack of respect, one more in an already long list." A moment later I was asked to leave. I had already managed to send my post into this wide open space, where no one asks me to show my passport.

Request list

My friend Yuslemi's pocketbook hasn't recovered from the last meeting at her son's primary school. Part of the parent-teacher meeting was dedicated to classroom needs, and in particular, what each family needed to come up with to buy a much-needed fan. The question of cleaning occupied about twenty minutes, and each parent made a note of various products, such as detergent, a floor mop, and a broom, that he or she needed to bring. With five pesos a month from each student, a lady could be paid to clean the room once a week.

The school lacks cleaning staff because the wages are too low. The person they will illegally contract with will probably be a retiree with no labor protection, no vacations, and no sick pay.

When that meeting was over, it was time for another. Was there a father who could repair broken chairs? A gentleman raised his hand. Another offered to supply a padlock for the door, and a mom committed to print out the math tests given in late January. Without a copier, reproduction of the tests falls to a parent who works at a State enterprise with an available copier. Everything was agreed upon in an atmosphere of business-as-usual, and the teacher declared the meeting a success.

Revolution.com

In the closed room of the Palace of Conventions, an Information Technology conference, accessible only to foreign delegates or credentialed Cubans, ended today, February 13. As much as I tried to slip into the event, I lacked the official institutional backing required to be there. In an optimistic preamble to the meeting, the Vice Minister of Informatics and Communications gave an interview to the newspaper *Juventud Rebelde*. Full of vague statements about the future, he renewed—in some—hopes for broad access to the Internet. But after reading this functionary's comments, I'm more alarmed than comforted.

He did not offer the slightest criticism of censorship or the blocking of pages that is so common on Cuban networks. He put ideological differences on a long list of atrocities including, "incitements to terrorism, xenophobia, pornography…" and added, "of course, inciting subversion of the established order in Cuba, and frankly counterrevolutionary content." The final adjective confirms for me that universal access will continue to be denied due to criteria that have nothing to do with bandwidth or satellite connections.

But it's not worth getting upset about. The Internet will not be a crumb that falls from above, a privilege earned by good conduct, or a benefit given in exchange for applauding. Not this time. A true revolution.com is taking place, parallel and contrary to the rationing they want to impose on the virtual world. There are no bearded ones, no rifles, much less a leader shouting from the platform. It is slow, but it will reach nearly all Cubans. Its commanders carry strange names like Gmail, Wordpress, Skype and Facebook: They do not create divisions but rather unite people.

The effect of this technological revolution will last more than fifty years; there is little that ministers, digital filters, or false promises of access for all can do to prevent or impede it. Even today, while they hold the closing ceremony of Information Technology 2009 behind closed doors, there is a new opening somewhere through which we can pass without permission.

Gratitude and a request

I don't want to let another day pass continuing in my ingratitude, not thanking the "selfless companions" who monitor the entrance to my building. They, through their great sacrifice in the last few weeks, have managed to limit the acts of vandalism so common in this building. No one has stolen clothes from the clotheslines; we haven't found any human excrement on the stairs; no exhibitionist has exposed himself to some startled teenager; the dominoes table has been suspended until further notice, and even the vagabond dogs have avoided doing their thing down there.

All this is thanks to the rotating shifts maintained by two disciplined members of the Ministry of the Interior— to keep an eye on me—in the lobby of my concrete block.

Along with my infinite gratitude, I just want to ask them, please, turn a blind eye to illegal vendors. No one—not even a distributor of cockroach poison—has been shouting his wares in our hallways. I feel I'm to blame for the commercial strangulation of the other 143 apartments, and I must do something to relieve them. So, I ask them, these soldiers of MININT lying in wait for their prey—look the other way when it comes to the food vendors. This doesn't have to be the siege of Lisbon!

Between the two walls

Today, Februaray 17 at 3:00, we managed to present Orlando Luís Pardo Lazo's novel *Boring Home* during the International Book Fair. After sneaking through the alleys of Cerro to lose the two "securities" following us, we came out at the Capitol and took a bus through the tunnel under the bay. Tension, fear, and doubt joined us on this brief trip to the La Cabaña fortress. Orlando was thinking of his mother, with her high blood pressure, frightened by threatening phone calls. I was thinking of Teo at school, unaware that perhaps no one would be there when he got home. Fortunately, the fears were only phantoms.

We understood later that the police operation was

meant to intimidate, but there was little they could do in front of the foreign press or international writers. Sitting on the grass, we began speaking to a group of fifteen people and ended with applause from more than forty. We were surprised by the presence and solidarity of several young writers and poets who are published by the official Cuban publishing house. We were also surprised by some Latin American novelists who supported us with words and hugs. Gorki and Ciro of the punk rock band Porno Para Ricardo attended, Claudia Cadelo of the blog *Octavo Cerco*, Lía Villares, author of the blog *Habanemia*, Reinaldo Escobar, blogger of *Desde Aqui*, the photographer Claudio Madan and others I won't mention so as not to cause them harm.

From across the street they used a telephoto lens to film everything happening on that green esplanade. Several primary schools had been invited to fly kites in the same spot, and a raucous reggaeton concert started exactly at three. However, we managed to isolate ourselves from all that and enter the door of *Boring Home*, to raise ourselves a few centimeters above the dusty reality of the watched and the watchers.

From where I was sitting, the wall of La Cabaña looked even more deteriorated, full of openings, small porosities in the stone.

Take me sailing on the wide sea[16]

In a land surrounded by water, the sailor is the link to the other side, the bearer of images that the islander cannot see. In the case of Cuba, someone who works on a ship can also buy abroad many products unavailable in local markets. He is a kind of Ulysses who, after months at sea, brings home a suitcase full of trinkets for the family. The sailor brings household appliances for the black market and makes fashions arrive earlier than planned by the bureaucrats of domestic commerce.

For several decades, to be a "merchant seaman" was to belong to a select fraternity that could go beyond the horizon and bring things never seen in these latitudes. The first jeans, tape recorders, and chewing gum I ever saw were transported by these lucky crew members. It was the same with digital clocks, color televisions and some cars that bore no resemblance to the unattractive Russian Ladas and Moskoviches.

For the relatives of a sailor, the long months of absence are soothed by an economic balm. When sailors drop anchor and retire, they can live on what they've managed to transport and on the images that remain in their memories.

I am telling this whole story of boats, masts, and the informal market because of Oscar, the husband of the blogger of *Sin Evasion*, who they are threatening to expel from his job as a sailor. The motive: Miriam Celaya's decision to drop her mask and to continue writing her opinions. The punishment: Leaving the family without support. For her to navigate freely on the Web, he may lose his chance to sail the waters.

A macho discourse

I still remember the odor of the gas masks we wore, running

to the shelter during military practice at primary school. My classmates and I feared that one day we'd run to shelter in the basement while bombs fell outside. Today, the city shows traces of a constant attack by the projectiles of mismanagement and the bullets of a centralized economy. In all that time, preparing for a battle that never came, we overlooked the fact that the main confrontation was occurring amongst ourselves: A prolonged battle between those fed up with warmongering and those who needed "a place under siege, where dissent is treason."

Several generations of Cubans came of age surrounded by billboards warning of possible invasion from the north. Calls to resist—though nobody knows exactly against what or whom—remain a constant undercurrent. Like a soldier sleeping with one eye open, ready to jump up at the trumpet's call, we too must always be on edge. But actually, indifference won the key battle, and most of my childhood friends ended up going into exile rather than the trenches.

After decades of hearing the same thing, I'm tired of this "macho" wrapped in an olive-green uniform; of the adjective "virile" associated with bravery; of hairy chests having the greater say. This female waits to switch to words such as: prosperity, reconciliation, harmony, and coexistence.

Of equinoxes and grandchildren

They took Adolfo one morning six years ago, raiding his home as if he were a dangerous terrorist. There were neither weapons nor chemical substances in his poor home in

Central Havana, but his papers bore witness to many opinions expressed in writing without permission.

They indicted him with the same urgency that—in
those same days—they shot three young men for hijacking
a boat to go to Florida. It was near the equinox, but to us
it seemed so dark we could only call it one thing: The Black
Spring of 2003. Not even the war in Iraq managed to obscure the news of the seventy-five prisoners taken. The old
trick of taking advantage of everyone's looking the other
way, so often and successfully repeated, didn't work this
time.

From his prison in Ciego de Ávila, Adolfo called to tell
us that his daughter Joana is going to have a baby. He probably won't be able to see this baby get its first tooth. His
release has been turned into a bargaining chip in a political game, and no one knows how or when it will be played.
Only one man, who is dying and therefore stubborn, seems
to have the ability to allow his release from prison. For that
fading old man, the future of Adolfo—free and living in a
plural Cuba—must hurt more than the needles of serums.
Despite the enormous power of this octogenarian patient,
he will not be able prevent that, one day, this humble English professor's grandchild will see him as just another
name in the history books, as the capricious *caudillo* who
put his grandfather behind bars.

As it turns out, March is not the month when days last
as long as nights, because a persistent eclipse of freedom
has settled over us. I watch and wait, but we continue in
this penumbra. Far ahead, I manage to see my children and
those of Joana, under a persistent light, calling to us.

The shredder

When you read this post I will be sitting among military uniforms in the waiting room of the Plaza Municipality Office of Immigration and Emigration. I am waiting for a permit to travel that has already been denied twice. Over the last year, obedient soldiers dedicated to limiting our freedom of movement have not permitted me to accept international invitations. In their databases next to my name must be a mark condemning me to island confinement. In the logic of this Daddy-State it is normal that I should be punished for writing a blog and denied the "white card" needed to travel—like a box on the ears—for believing myself a free person.

My greatest hope for this bureaucratic Friday is that someone will put a hand on my shoulder and say, "We were wrong about you, you can leave." But I don't think they will amend the "error" of blocking my travel, nor do I harbor the slightest hope of boarding an airplane on March 29. But I will sit in the crowded lobby of the mansion at Seventeenth and K for two reasons: to inconvenience them with my pigheadedness and to claim my rights. To show them visas authorizing my entry into other countries, while they alone curb my travel. I will sit, confident that one day all this machinery to extract profits and generate ideological loyalties will cease to exist.

I do confess, I don't want the right to travel given as a gift. Rather, I fantasize that—this very day—while I am waiting for my third "No," someone will come and announce that regulations blocking travel were just repealed. But I have a feeling that I will leave Cuba when everyone can leave freely, and not before. In the meantime, I will continue to besiege them with my demands, my posts, and my questions.

Third time is not a charm

This time they were more direct: "You are not authorized to travel," the woman, dressed in her olive-green, told me quietly, almost nicely. My third bid for permission to leave ended without much delay and with the same negative response. I demanded an explanation from the officer, but she was only a intermediary between me and her hidden bosses.

While they were telling me "No," I recalled the declarations made by Miguel Barnet a couple of months ago.[17] The president of the Cuban Writers and Artists Union (UNEAC) affirmed that all Cubans could travel, except those who have a debt to the justice system. I spent the day searching for some legal reason hanging over me, but nothing came to mind. Even the rice cooker I bought on credit at the ration store is paid for in full—though it only worked for two months before it completely broke down.

I have never been charged in court, yet I am condemned not to leave this Island. This restriction has not been dictated by a judge, nor could I have appealed it to jury, rather it comes from the Great Prosecutor, who has set himself up as the Cuban State.

That same severe magistrate determined that the old woman sitting next to me would not receive the "white card" because her son "deserted" from a medical mission. The boy who waited in the corner couldn't travel either, because his athlete father now plays under a different flag. The list of the punished is so long and the reasons so varied that we would make a huge group of forced "stay-at-homes." Too bad the vast majority are still silent in the hopes that one day they'll be allowed to leave, like one rewarded for good behavior.

Perhaps those who are denied exit permits should visit the office of the naïve president of UNEAC. Maybe he can explain to us the crime for which we've been condemned.

And they gave us the microphones...

An unforgettable night yesterday, March 29, at the Wilfredo Lam Center, thanks to performance artist Tania Bruguera. A podium with microphones, in front of an enormous red curtain, set the stage for the interactive installation in the central courtyard. Anyone who wanted to could use the podium, for just one minute, to deliver any rousing speech he or she pleased.

As microphones are rare here—I certainly never encountered any in my time as a Young Pioneer reciting patriotic verses—I took the opportunity. Advised ahead of time by friends, I had prepared a speech on freedom of expression, censorship, blogs, and that elusive tool that is the Internet. In front of national television cameras and protected by the foreign guests at the Tenth Havana Biennial, my minute was followed by shouts of "Freedom," "Democracy," and even open challenges to Cuban authorities. I remember one boy of twenty who confessed that he had never felt more free.

Tania gave us the microphones, we who have suffered, under the hot sun, the speechifying of others, unable to speak ourselves. It was an artistic action, but there was no entertainment in our declarations. Everyone was very serious. A dove rested on our shoulders—probably not as well-trained as the one that landed on our new Leader fifty years ago. However, none of us who spoke considered ourselves chosen. And none wanted to stay—for fifty years—shouting into microphones.

The silent press

Flooded with commemorations and dates to be celebrated, we didn't pay much attention to Cuban Press Day, March 14. The news featured long reports about the selfless efforts of journalists and their loyalty to the Revolution. Some reporters received certificates for outstanding work and impeccable ideological positions, while *Granma* devoted a ton of space to self-congratulation.

At the same time, US President Barack Obama eased limitations on travel to the Island for Cuban Americans. The restrictions he abolished had prevented these immigrants from visiting their families more than once every three years, and there had also been a strict limit on sending remittances to relatives on the Island. For the precarious domestic economy, money sent from the United States is oxygen for survival. In a country where so many citizens live on the opposite shore, notice of Obama's actions should have been front-page news everywhere. It was what the journalism schools teach as the "obligatory lead."

However, the Cuban press barely mentioned this positive step by the White House. An official silence was the only response to this long-awaited and welcome measure. In the streets, no one talked about anything else. Mothers prepared to welcome their children living in the North, but the official media remained wary. Journalists are caught up in other issues: the potato harvest, the World Baseball Classic, the Bolivarian Revolution and, of course, the celebrations of Cuban Press Day.

Completed performance

Without the statement by Tenth Havana Biennial Organizing Committee about the event at the Wilfredo Lam Center on Sunday, March 29, Tania Bruguera's performance wouldn't have been complete. For a moment of freedom at a microphone, it was fitting punishment. Without their rebuke, the performance would have seemed like a signal that intolerance had yielded; that it was now possible to mount a podium and express oneself without fear.

We should be grateful to those who wrote the insulting tirade in *La Jirabilla*.[18] Without it, everything would seem to be in the realm of the permitted, a performance designed to give the appearance of openness.

With those five paragraphs they closed—in the best possible way—her piece. They reminded us, those of us rash enough to take advantage of the brief moment of freedom, that punishment and rebuke remain in place. The Organizing Committee has confirmed, in its text full of insults, why so many cries of freedom came from the podium.

With its accusations, it has exposed the reason why many more didn't dare—that night—to take the microphone.

Instant teachers

Among my son's friends is one particularly apathetic boy who is about to finish basic secondary school. He cares little for books, and it's been a headache for his parents to get him to the ninth grade. A week ago I learned that he was heading for a career as a teacher. I thought they must be talking about another boy, because the one I know lacks any aptitude for teaching. When I asked his reasons, he answered my doubts by explaining, "I'm going to study to be a teacher because they study in the city and I don't want to go to a boarding school in the country."

A very high percentage of those who choose teaching— I would venture to guess nearly all of them—do so because they have no other option. They are the students who, because of bad grades, can't aspire to a computer specialty or to a high school for hard sciences. After less than three years' training, they will be standing at a chalkboard in front of students nearly their own age. Without these "instant teachers" there would be no instructors at all. Miserable salaries have driven qualified teachers to better-paying occupations.

It scares me when I think of young people studying under this boy. I live in terror of hearing my grandchildren say, "The star in the Cuban flag has five points because it represents the five Cuban agents in US prisons," or that "Madagascar is an island in South America." I'm not exaggerating;

we hear tons of anecdotes like this from parents of children taught by "instant" teachers. If such a noble profession continues to be filled by the least qualified, the educational level of generations to come will be very poor. Already a teacher confessed to my son and his classmates, when they started seventh grade, "Study hard so you won't end up like me. I had to become a teacher because of my bad grades."

Feast envy

A PowerPoint presentation now circulating details the closure of a famous restaurant in Havana. The sequence of photos, apparently taken by the Department of Technical Investigations, the financial police, shows the "evidence" used to charge Juan Carlos Fernandez Garcia, owner of the *paladar,* or private restaurant, Hurón Azul. I stopped looking at the rudimentary multimedia show out of disgust, not because of the goods shown there.

The list of Juan Carlos's "crimes" are: selling "prohibited food" such as lobster and beef; having more than twelve seats in the restaurant; giving credit to artists to eat there; becoming a patron of the arts; paying a huge electricity bill; having a lot of cash; and—what nerve—wanting to open a restaurant in Milan.

Wouldn't it be easier just to authorize the sale of the crustaceans that live in our sea, to congratulate Juan Carlos for his work promoting culture, and to allow each *paladar* to have however many chairs and employees it needs?

No, because to authorize all that would set off competition with the inefficient restaurants and cultural centers owned by the State. To allow Hurón Azul to continue to grow would be to run the risk that its proprietor might one day want to found an art magazine or open a museum to show off his private collection.

I feel sorry for whoever took these photos. I can see, in the careful focus on the food, the deep poverty of whoever prepared the dossier. I'm deeply ashamed that police in my country are dedicated to imprisoning enterprising citizens, while the streets are full of criminals who snatch purses, steal, and defraud. I'm sad for my neighbors, green with envy, who begrudge Juan Carlos his prosperity. Above all, I think about the old gentleman who looked after the cars at the *paladar* entrance, and the lady who washed the dishes, now without work, and especially Juan Carlos's children. But possibly they understand, given the example of the Hurón Azul, that to prosper one must get off this Island.

The seven passing by Thebes

The visit of seven members from the United States Congress intensifies hopes for an avalanche of American tourists. Owners of rooms for rent calculate potential earnings, and taxi drivers dream of those who chew gum and leave generous tips. At Terminal Two in José Martí Airport, some have already arrived. People have nicknamed these early visitors "the brave ones." I don't know if it's for the risk they run with regard to the laws of their own country, or because of their audacity in coming to an Island where, according to the official version, they are "the enemy."

The expected "normalization of relations between Cuba

and the United States" must occur mainly between the two administrations. At the level of the people, we've been in agreement for some time, and it is only our leaders who fail to realize that our nation is bi-territorial, given the large number of our compatriots living in the United States. Thus, the Cuban side is very interested in keeping relations flowing across the Florida Straits. However, it seems that Obama, not Raúl, will take the first step.

I have difficulty calling to mind a single day in these last fifty years when Cubans weren't warned that our powerful neighbor was thinking of invading us. What will happen to the slogan, *Cuba Si! Yankees No!*, to the shouts of *Gringos!* when we are all greeting them here so cordially?

Most of the political speeches of the last fifty years will be passé, and there won't be any bogeyman with which to frighten the children. What will the party militants think if they're ordered to accept those whom, until recently, they hated? How can David look good in the photos if, instead of using stone and the slingshot, he sits down to talk to Goliath?

Interestingly, I don't see anyone in the streets upset about these changes. The nervousness is only among those who have used the confrontation to stay in power. Rather, I observe the joy, the hope, the vague sense that the distance between Miami and Havana might become smaller and more familiar.

Montagues and Capulets

What was the origin of the feud between Romeo and

Juliet's families? I remember the scaling of the balcony, the promises to return, the banishment to Mantua, but I can't remember the spark that set off the confrontation between the two clans. Many young Cubans, like Shakespeare's lovers, have been born into a conflict they barely understand. They grew up in the shadow of the feud between the Cuban and US governments, nursed on the resentments of their parents and grandparents.

Today, those under thirty look ahead, and it seems normal that some day Montagues and Capulets will mix blood in a common offspring, overcoming swords and poisons. We won't be able to prevent them from loving each other; let us, then, prevent them from simulating a hatred they don't feel, and especially from feigning suicide to please their elders.

And now what?

The ball is in Cuba's court after Obama's announcement yesterday, April 14, of new flexibility in his policies toward Cuba. The players on this side seem a bit confused—hesitating between grabbing the ball, abusing it, or simply ignoring it. The timing couldn't be better: loyalty to the government has never seemed more perverse and ideological fervor never as feeble. On top of that, few still believe the story that our powerful neighbor will attack us, and the majority feel that this impasse has gone on too long.

The next move is up to Raúl Castro, but we have the sense we will be left waiting. The ball we would like him to throw would open spaces for citizens' initiatives, permit free association and, in a gesture of political honesty, put him to the test of genuinely free elections. He should "decriminalize political dissent" and immediately annul the long prison sentences of those punished for differences of opinion. In a bold move, "the permanent second" should dare to offer more than just an olive branch. We are hoping that he will eliminate the travel restrictions, which would put an end to the extortionate business of permits and allow us to come and go freely from the Island.

The game would be more dynamic if he passed the Cuban people the ball of change. Many would kick it to end censorship, State control over information, ideological selection in certain professions, indoctrination in education, and the punishment of those who think differently. We would kick it to be able to surf the Internet without blocked websites, to be able to say the word "freedom" into an open microphone without being accused of "a counterrevolutionary provocation."

Many of us have already climbed down from the bleachers. If the Cuban government doesn't grab the ball, there are thousands of hands ready to take a turn at launching it.

To the outside world

The Summit of the Americas ended yesterday, April 20, and it doesn't appear that an urgent meeting of the Cuban parliament, or a special plenary session of the Party Central Committee, is being convened to discuss the proposals made by Obama. "A fresh start with Cuba," the American president said in Trinidad and Tobago, but today, Fidel

Castro's *Reflections* referred only to Daniel Ortega's long speech. The *National News* hasn't gone into the street to ask people's opinions, and my neighbor has been drafted into Operation Caguairan to prepare for a possible invasion from the North.

Given the importance of what's going on, the "accountability meeting" that my building is holding today should be devoted to the new relations between Cuba and the United States. But the delegate prefers to talk about unruly neighbors who throw trash outside the bins, rather than ask what we think about the end of the long dispute. In my son's school some teacher repeats that "Obama is like Bush, but painted black," and the billboards in the street still call for continuing the struggle against imperialism.

I don't know what to think, given the difference between what they say to the outside world and the tiresome sermons they address to us. Even Raúl Castro seems ready to talk to Obama about things he's never wanted to discuss with us. I can't help but ask myself: Is all this talk of "olive branches" and discussions of general measures just words addressed to the outside world? Phrases they will only pronounce far from our ears?

A kitchen chorus

Old pots and pans used to feed the family can be transformed into a kind of ballot, one we can't leave in the box, and into the hand we dare not raise in the assembly. Any object can serve, if given the required space: A piece of fabric hung from the balcony, a newspaper waved in public, a pot banged along with others. The great metallic choir made up of spoons and pans could be—on May first at 8:30—our voice, to say what is stuck in our throats.

Restrictions on coming to and going from Cuba have lasted too long. So I will bang my pot for my parents, who have never been able to cross the sea that separates us from the world, and also for myself, forced for the last two years to travel only in the virtual world. I will pound out a rhythm thinking of Teo, condemned to permanent exile if he happens to board a plane before the age of eighteen. I will beat the drum for Edgar, still on a hunger strike after seven denials of his request for permission to leave. At the end of the metal concert I will dedicate a couple of notes to Marta, who didn't get the "white card" to see her grand-daughter born in Florida.

After so much beating, the bottom of the pan probably won't serve for frying even one more egg. But for the nec-essary "food" to travel, move about freely, and leave home without permission, it's well worth breaking all the pots and pans in my kitchen.

Trivialities

While the dismissal of Carlos Lage and Felipe Perez Roque was grabbing headlines and generating rumors, Xiomara was worrying about something much closer to home. For the past four months, in her town of Pinar del Rio, the sani-tary napkins haven't come. She and her daughters cut up a couple of sheets and managed to make some pads, which they washed after each use. If the ration market lacks feminine hygiene products, the already small number of towels and pillowcases remaining in Cuban households will shrink even further. Mother Nature does not understand the mechanisms of distribution, and so, every twenty-eight days, she puts those mechanisms to the test.

Xiomara recounted, with the shame of speaking publicly about something she would prefer to keep private, that the other workers at her company had the same problem. "Because of this we might refuse to go to work," she told me. I imagined a "Strike of the Period," a massive protest marked by the cycle of ovulation.

Nothing in the province of Pinar del Rio, however, stops for this "triviality." Officials continue to speak of "recovering from the hurricanes" and the newspapers—which unfortunately cannot be used as sanitary pads—talk about exceeding the goals of the potato harvest. The drama is hidden in the bathrooms and expressed in two new wrinkles on some women's brows.

There are those who think that the dismissal of officials, or a merger of ministries, is the road to real change. I feel, however, that the triggering spark of transformation could simply be a group of women tired of washing out, every month, rags for their menstrual cycles.

Not under pressure... nor without pressure

This morning, April 27, some of us went with our friend Edgar to appeal his denial of permission to leave the country. A few steps from the Office of Legal Counsel is the site of the National Immigration and Emigration office. I already know the place, having been there just a year ago with a similar appeal, which ended with a confirmation that I could not travel "for the moment." Uniformed officers and people quietly hoping to have their cases revisited inhabit the stage at this branch of the Ministry of the Interior.

The signatures collected from Cubans here and outside the country were handed over to the duty officer, who confirmed that the Ministry now has sixty days to respond to his request. On Friday, two Section 21 officers had "suggested" to Edgar that he not appear here today. The implication was that if he were quiet, they would allow him to travel by August. After this young man's hunger strike, "the boys of the apparatus" informed him, immigration officials couldn't be seen to "act under pressure" in letting him on the plane.

As if it weren't completely common that citizens bring pressure to bear and politicians amend their actions accordingly. As if it were not for precisely this reason that they occupy their positions—to yield, again and again, to the demands of society. Hasn't it been said by enough voices that requiring permission to leave and enter Cuba must be repealed? What more has to happen?

Newsletter

Several friends and I have started a small information service through SMS texting. News not mentioned in the official media is sent via cell phone to one group of people, who then send it on to others. This may seem like a limited network—because the number of Cubans with cell phones is small—but I have a lot of faith in its potential. It's enough that someone would like to pass on a headline to another interested person for this new information pathway to grow.

I think we should continue to develop this rough "news service." Perhaps those who want to help could create a website where we can leave our cell phone numbers and get the news for free. We live in a country where distributing an actual newspaper can result in being charged with the crime of "enemy propaganda," so the virtual pathways need to be strengthened... at least while there is no new law to prohibit them.

Already we have a small group of Cubans using mobiles to expand our sources of information. This little accessory could well become the source of the news that we're missing at the newsstands.

May Day

Yesterday was an intense day. There was a parade in the morning, a heavy rain shower in the afternoon, and a few upstarts banging pots and pans at 8:30 in the evening. The turnout at the Plaza of the Revolution looked the same as always, the rain was just as wet, and the kitchen chorus's banging was an unusual symphony of a few.

From my terrace, we heard little reaction to the first bangs on the pot, but we have the joy of knowing that they heard us from a long way off. From a quick phone survey I know that in Pinar del Rio they too heard the sound of banging metal, while several neighborhoods in Havana remained silent. The limited drumming came from a few individuals who dared, and not from the robotic many who paraded in the morning. Such is the difference between an unprompted chirp-chirp and crowing under orders.

Every spark is small, I told someone who asked me about last night and in its debut, a tool of expression is used timidly. When I heard about the call circulating on the Internet, I met with several friends who thought the simple gesture of turning off the lights would be better. Making noise involves exposing oneself too much, and there are many people who still fear reprisals. Making the house dark, they reasoned, can be done without leaving evidence and is a gesture our citizens are ready to make.

Despite how few notes were heard, I think it changed something about International Workers' Day—this faint banging of spoons on tin after the first downpour of May.

Skeptical grandchildren

I go wandering with my youngest grandson through the streets of a Havana both different and familiar. I don't have a blog anymore, and my seventy years show in every wrinkle and in my long white braid. Even though this could be a dark, futuristic fantasy, I prefer to believe that we are walking through a reborn and prosperous city. We come to the park to sit in the sun, and I try—like old people every-where—to tell him about "my day," those years when I was thin and had his energy.

Spanish is his mother tongue, but the boy looks at me as if he doesn't understand a word I say. He casts a doubtful glance my way when I refer to the "Special Period," "the ration book," "rationed products," and "ideological loyalty." His problems are so different, how could he understand those I once had? Without embarrassment he shows some historical confusion, calling a dead leader by the name of a salsa singer. He's unable to tell the difference between a speech decreeing the triumph of the socialist Revolution and one which announced the collapse of the Soviet Union.

Out of respect he doesn't tell me to be quiet, but I can see that my chatter bores him. "Grandma is stuck in the past," he'll say when I leave, but to my face he pretends to listen to my ancient anecdotes about a far-off Cuba. This boy doesn't know that the promise of his existence allowed me to maintain my sanity forty years ago. Anticipating his sitting with an expression of disbelief on a park bench in a future Havana kept me from taking the way of the sea, of pretending, of silence. I've made it here thanks to him. And instead of telling him that, I bore him with my anecdotes about what happened, about things that will never happen again.

One step forward, two steps back

I've gone a couple of days without connecting to the Internet. There's a new complication for alternative bloggers. In order to connect to the Web, hotels now demand that you prove you live outside Cuba. The desk clerks tell me—though they are just as native as I am—that that blue residence card will not allow me to dive into the vast World Wide Web. "It's a decision that comes from above," one tells me, as if this type of decision happens not in government offices but somewhere over their heads.

I see it's going to be hard to change myself into a foreigner overnight, so the only thing left is to protest and publicize this new apartheid. I will go back disguised as a tourist, but this time I will have to learn a language as complicated as Hungarian to fool the access-card sellers. Maybe I can prowl around the hotels and ask a foreigner to buy me this forbidden entrance key, this safe conduct to "not be Cuban."

Rainbow in the blogosphere

Since I started writing *Generation Y* in April 2007 much has changed in the "Made in Cuba" blogosphere, there are now more of us and fewer who hide behind a pseudonym. We've managed to join together beyond the virtual world, too—proof being the Blogger Journey that we continue every week.

Saturday was Pinar del Rio's turn, where the "restless boys" of State Security had prevented us traveling in December. Wordpress, the free software installed on my blog, was the main character in the weekend's exercises. And a good part of our discussion revolved around the trick of slipping into hotels or cybercafés—an area where I have a lot of experience. In Pinar del Rio, west of Havana, there are no other possibilities for Internet access, except for a few controlled networks at state institutions. So, among the most-discussed topics was how to maintain publication frequency in a province so disconnected from the Web.

I returned to Havana with the feeling that the blogosphere will grow exponentially in coming months. For me, a pioneer in this adventure, there is no greater happiness than to see the rise of so many different and free spaces.

Hard shell

Tolerance of private transportation operators has lasted too long. For two years this has been the most commonly known change of Raúl Castro's government—though the foreign press paid more attention to permission to buy a computer, open a cell phone account, or rent a hotel room. Tolerance of unauthorized drivers is more important to our daily lives than any of these new services available only in convertible currency.

But last Friday, few shared taxis were on the street. New regulations now require a special license. I fear that this new rule will reduce the mobility of thousands of people, though not of the elite who can pay ten Cuban pesos—a day's wages—to go from Central Havana to the municipality of Playa. These old cars move people of all classes—from the student who needs to be on time to class, to the retiree going to visit his grandchildren in Mantilla, to the musician heading to his gig in a nightclub.

These *almendrones* make up for what public transportation lacks: Reliability, frequency, and good access to all areas of the country.[19] They've outlived the many attempts to rehabilitate the state-owned bus system. They've survived strict controls, obligatory payoff's to the cops, restrictions on buying spare parts, and the high price of fuel. These

vehicles, with their hard shells, keep rolling through the
city. We hope their stubborn frames will be shockproof
against the new rulings.

Blogger "sit-in"

I'm starting to believe that the influence of the Internet on
our reality is even greater than I had thought.

After several days of not being allowed to connect in
hotels—the Meliá Cohiba, the Panorama, and the emblem-
atic Hotel Nacional—the ban appears to have been lifted.
Today I spoke with the same clerks who, two weeks ago,
showed me the resolution excluding Cubans from accessing
the Web. Today, they told me I can buy the blessed card that
unlocks the door to the virtual world.

This may sound a bit boastful, but I think that if we had
not raised a ruckus—denouncing this segregation—we
would still be deprived of the ability to connect. Yes, they
cede when we push back, when citizens raise their voices
and the international media hears the echo. We need to
make the most of this situation, now that they are saying
"Cubans can connect." We must hold them to it. If they try
to shut us out again there will always be Twitter, Facebook,
and text messages to launch our protest.

Bucket and pitcher

Under the sink is the plastic bucket with which the entire
family bathes. It's been over twenty years since the pipes
collapsed, and to use the bathroom they have to carry

water from a tank on the patio. In winter they prepare a lukewarm bath thanks to an electrical heater made from two condensed-milk cans. None of the children knows the sensation of a jet of water falling on shoulders. Since water comes only once a week, no one can waste it on a shower.

To the rhythm of a pitcher rising and falling, the majority of people I know groom themselves. Deterioration of the water system and the high price of plumbing parts contributes to the calamitous state of the toilets. Just washing one's body, which should be an intimate and pleasant activity, is, for most of my compatriots, a series of inconveniences. To this poor state of infrastructure we must add that buying shampoo and soap requires a currency different from that in which we are paid.

Film genre

One day my father came home pale and trembling. He had just seen a video—shown only to Communist Party members—announcing the cuts of the "Special Period." Sitting at the table, he told us that hardship could reach the dreaded "Zero Option," where a single collective pot would have to feed all the neighbors on the block. The film my dad saw that night was only for people of "proven" ideology.

Only a "revolutionary elite" seems to have the right to know about issues that concern all citizens. I thought this practice had passed with the 1970s and '80s, but now there is a new secret video playing. This new movie is about the downfall of Carlos Lage and Philip Perez Roque, the two most recently devoured by power. They are not heroes, but rather victims, scapegoats in something more like a Greek tragedy than an action thriller.

Everyone's whispering about the scenes in which both these ex-civil servants insult the generation in power, but so far, no copy of the video has been leaked. Cubans are waiting for a generous hand to steal the film and circulate it on our alternative networks. Gone are the days when something like this can be kept among the faithful; technology knows nothing of classified material or news only for the select.

My father called yesterday to see if I'd seen the film. "Don't worry," I told him, "as soon as I have it, I'll show it to you," and I immediately remembered when he broke with Party orders to warn us of what was to come.

Written in our genes

After five attempts to leave illegally, Carlos has found a way without the danger of sharks and sunstroke. He will leave Cuba via one of the few countries that don't demand a visa. Thousands of young people have left this way in the last few months after realizing that the government's announced "process of change" was just more of the same.

This recidivist rafter is now over thirty years old and has spent at least a third of his life with eyes focused on the far shore, but if everything goes well, he will be looking at the Island from a distance in just a couple of months.

Every year I'm in the sad position of having to remake my group of friends because, as Wendy Guerra says, "Everyone's left," even those who planned to grow old here or had some economic advantage that allowed them to live comfortably. Even my friend who seemed to intend—like me—to let the old El Morro lighthouse go dark once everyone else was gone has told us he's leaving. He came to the house yesterday, whispering, as if he was afraid the apartment was bugged, and said, "I can't take it any more." The phrase I've heard so often.

He leaves despite a good apartment, a job that pays well, and an active social life. He made the decision to emigrate for reasons very different from Carlos's, but they both agree they don't want their children to be born in Cuba. One lives in his grandmother's falling-down house, the other sleeps each night with the air conditioner set to 20 degrees Celsius. Their lives are so different and their aspirations so similar that I can only think the imperative to emigrate is in our genes—a pull from within, the instinct for self-preservation that tells us, "Save yourselves, get out of here."

When the KGB fights the CIA, the police always win

Today is not the first time I've heard that MSN Messenger is blocked for Cuban users. Almost three years ago, a friend furtively snuck me into her workplace so I could connect to the Internet. I was missing some data for an article I wanted to write, so I asked for a few minutes with an old computer. This was back when I was pretending to be a tourist to get online in hotels, and that week I didn't have the convertible pesos to pay for the hour of access.

My friend read the list of prohibited sites, and added that MSN had been blocked for months. "You can't use any e-mail or chat services that aren't local," and "don't even think about going to *El Nuevo Herald*," she said, eyes wide. When I asked about the block on the Microsoft software, she explained that I should not use any interface that network administrators couldn't control. Hotmail was banned because it was almost impenetrable to the recording software that kept a record of all the employees' correspondence. A little later, Yahoo and Gmail would also be banned for the same reason.

Now the ban is coming from the other side, from those whose programs help us escape government control: "Windows Live Messenger IM has been disabled for users in countries embargoed by the United States," reads the note from Microsoft announcing the cutoff. Once again, we citizens lose out. Our government already has its own channels for communicating with the world. This is clearly a blow to us Web renegades—meaning nearly everyone who accesses the Internet from Cuba. The censor at the company where my friend works must be delighted: Microsoft just did his work for him.

The advantage of a snack

I'd like to propose an ode to the daily snack received by custodians and security personnel at certain state offices. A ham-and-cheese roll with a soft drink is the reason thousands of Cubans are still at their jobs. Without the earnings from the resale of this refreshment, many would have abandoned their positions. In fact, one of the first questions when looking for employment is not salary—equally symbolic and inadequate everywhere—but rather, Is there a snack? Selling it for twenty Cuban pesos allows workers to double their income, though it means not eating.

Everywhere, discretely displayed but easy to find, are the bottles of TropiCola and the snack wrapped in cellophane. They're at the entrance of the telephone office, inside glass doors at the banks, in guard booths at ministries, in bus station ticket booths, inside museums, and even in the State cybercafé that offers slow Internet at high prices. Wherever there are custodians, escorts, and guards, they must resell their snack to stay on guard. A few slices of ham and cheese can make the difference between going to work in the morning and staying home.

What Poland left us

I was only fourteen and everything was happening much too fast around me. Shortages were severe and it was already difficult to find the magazines, with many colors but few truths, that came out of the USSR. We had seen the televised trial of General Ochoa and my parents lost their illusions watching the law cave before olive-green uniforms.[20]

News of Poland came in those same days. We didn't understand anything. Up until then, the European socialist bloc seemed like it would last forever. A distant cousin told us of her concerns after a brief stay in Moscow, but we still believed that the COMECON, the Warsaw Pact and the Robotron typewriters would outlive us all.

The word "Solidarity" had suddenly become fashionable. Although my Marxism-Leninism teacher made an effort to idealize the East, something inside him snapped when he learned what was happening on the streets of Warsaw. If the invasion of Czechoslovakia in 1968 had been difficult for our leaders to justify, the rebellion of the "Polish working class" left more than one person without answers.

I grew up, and had a son, and he, too, repeated the slogan, "Pioneers for communism, we will be like Che." Today he is the same age I was in that tumultuous year of 1989, when my doubts began; when I began to suspect that everything they'd drilled into me might not be true.

Doors that open, bars that shut

None of the various presidents who approved our island's readmission into the Organization of American States yesterday, June 4, were in office back in 1962, when we were expelled. However, the same people who governed my parents and grandparents are still in power here. The Cuban people have changed greatly in the meantime: Some died, others emigrated, and my generation—with its exotic "Y"— is starting to see its first gray hairs. But at the podium the same name has clung to the microphone all this time.

The OAS's decision presents our elders in power with an impossible dilemma—to choose between belligerence and harmony, which burns them like salt on a wound and drowns them as surely as water in their lungs. Because they live in the logic of confrontation, to them a possible seat in the OAS appears more dangerous than the barricades, where they are most comfortable. They know that taking the seat would put them inside a regional community that would support them, but it would also mean opening up the country.

Wednesday's announcement seems like another helping hand extended, a new door opened, only to have the government summarily reject it. John Paul II's desire, "Let Cuba open itself to the world, and let the world open itself to Cuba," would be accomplished if it weren't for the first part of that phrase. It seems those at the helm of my country prefer the catchy slogan shouted in the sixties, "With the OAS or without the OAS, we will win the fight." But now no one sees the fight anymore, the enemy fades, and the victory... ah, the victory... the victory is to have stayed in power all this time.

Red medalists

Among us there exists a frequently practiced sport, one whose stats and game times are not mentioned anywhere. This is the sport of surrendering the Communist Party card. It is a feat that many of my compatriots have spent years preparing for. Most important is to find the exact right moment to stand in front of the assembly and say, "*Compañeros*, for reasons of health I can't continue to perform the task you have assigned me." There are those who claim a sick mother, others who announce they are retiring to spend more time with their grandchildren. Few honestly confess that they've ceased to believe in the precepts and principles espoused by the Party.

I know someone who found a novel way out of the meetings, the unanimous votes, the calls for intransigence,

and the frequent mobilizations of the Cuban Communist
Party. Like a boxer, trained to endure until the sound of
the bell, he went to what would be his last Party meeting.
He surprised everyone with the novelty of his approach—
a jab from the left when no one expected it: "Every day I
buy things on the black market to feed my family, and as a
member of the Communist Party I should not be doing this.
Because I must choose between putting food on the table
or abiding by the discipline of this organization, I prefer to
resign." Everyone at the table looked at him with disbelief.
"But Ricardo, what are you talking about? Most of us here
buy on the black market." Then, the well-practiced knock-
out punch ended the brief round: "Ah... then I'm leaving
because I don't want to belong to a party of hypocrites, who
say one thing and do another."

He left the red book with his name and surname on the
table where he would never sit again. His wife gave him his
champion's medal when he returned home: "Finally, you
are free of the Party," she said, while planting a kiss and
handing him the towel.

A party without the guest of honor

A couple of days ago we held a small celebration with friends
because the new elevator installation was complete and a
party was definitely called for. For more than seven months
we had been climbing the stairs to our fourteenth floor. We
let everyone know there would be merrymaking until late,
and they all brought something to contribute to the fun. It
was a shame when they arrived, so tired and looking like

they had been cheated—because the flashing red lights
on the brand-new, recently installed Russian elevators announced, to one and all, that they were broken.

The officials who went to Russia to buy the equipment had decided that it wasn't necessary to spend the
extra money on lateral guides, a kind of track where the
car slides. They decided that old structures, installed more
than twenty-five years ago, were compatible with new
equipment. And so they began to install them. I will not
speak metaphorically or draw parallels between electrome-
chanics and politics, but applying innovative technology on
demonstrably wornout tracks sounds familiar...

The end result is little compatibility between the old
Soviet parts and the new Russian equipment, which now
makes horrifying noises as it goes up and down, in addition
to constantly breaking down. Officially, the installation is
finished; the plans are marked with the word "completed."
And soon the mechanics will be off to another building. We
continue using the stairs most of the time, and look like
clowns to our friends, who think our elevator inauguration
party was a joke in bad taste.

CUBALSE and Generation Motors

On June first, what everyone predicted was confirmed:
General Motors declared bankruptcy. National television
aired reports about the fallen giant, while in our streets,
old models from fifty years ago are still rolling. GM's tall sil-
ver tower became a symbol of the current global economic
crisis. Within Cuba there are other signs of these bad times:

Blackouts return, tourists are scarce, and public transport suffers another cutback. Here financial shares don't plummet, because they don't exist; companies hide their bankruptcies. Being state-owned, they don't have to report their finances to the public.

Another business conglomerate fell apart here, though the news avoided mentioning it. The powerful CUBALSE-has just disappeared.[21] It pioneered selling goods in convertible currency in a country where the majority is paid in Cuban pesos. Its employees seemed to be a mix of capitalist entrepreneurs and soldiers in a commercial army.

A discrete release detailed the dismemberment of the "Company for the Provision of Services to Foreigners," pieces of which went to other institutions. A whole structure of power, loyalties, and personal interests must have come crashing down when they announced the death of this "small giant." The requiem was played in hushed tones, however, so as not to unduly alarm us. We don't need to look at General Motors to conclude that this is happening not only abroad, but right here at home as well.

Newsletter

If there were an altar to technology I wouldn't hesitate to light a couple of candles. These cables, circuits, and chips have brought infinitely much more information, autonomy, and freedom to my life than that generated by the will of politicians or popular movements. This month marks the fifteenth anniversary of my building my first computer, which represented a one-hundred-and-eighty degree turn in my life. My hand is now a bit distorted from clutch-ing the mouse, most of the time I think as if I were de-signing for Dreamweaver, and I'm even tempted to press "control+alt+del" for a reset when I don't like what's going on around me.

And now a new service—sending out news reports via SMS—increases my faith in the power of these gadgets. Last week I learned about a site called *Granpa*—we hope it will be more objective than the Party's daily newspaper, *Granma*—that sends news to cell phones in Cuba. To start reading headlines on your cell, all you have to do is leave your phone number and choose what you'd like to receive.

The very best of luck to those who started this great idea—so necessary in these times we're living in. Since we don't have a real world paper to tell us what the official press keeps hidden, let me offer a big welcome to this news through electrical impulses, kudos for this flashing on my phone.

Taking note

What is happening in Iran now, and its peoples' use of the Internet, is a lesson for Cuban bloggers. Authorities here must also be making note of the dangers of Twitter, Face-book, and mobile phones. Seeing those young Iranians use all the technology they can to denounce injustice makes me think of everything we lack here on the island. The acid test of our virtual community has not yet arrived, but maybe it will surprise us tomorrow… despite the aggravation of low connectivity.

In our weekly blogger meetings, we watched a short video about Iranian cybernauts. I watched it again today in lieu of the images of the demonstrations that our official television refuses to show. I haven't seen the faces painted green, nor heard an announcer speak of the seven dead, but with this brief clip I can imagine everything. I can see an entire generation weary of the old structures, people—like me—who have ceased to believe in enlightened leaders who lead us like cattle. In the midst of all this are the bytes and the screens, and a new form of protest.

On days like this I so regret not being able to get online. I feel like I'm choking to have to wait to hear the news. If there's still time for me to extend my solidarity to the Iranian bloggers, then here is a post to tell them: "Today it's you, tomorrow it could well be us."

Nobody is listening

We've gone from one extreme to the other. Three years ago we had a president who would speak for hours in front of a microphone. Now we have a president who doesn't say a word.

I confess I prefer the restrained style, but there are a lot of explanations due, which, in the face of so much discontent, are urgent. Someone has to stand up and explain why wage reform failed, why the handovers of critical land grants were delayed, and why they haven't reduced the gap between the Cuban peso and the convertible currency.

Someone must tell us why eliminating the need for permission to travel outside Cuba was cancelled, and what

happened to reducing imports and to the so-called "business improvement program." The same voice that in 2007
declared there would be "a glass of milk for every Cuban"
needs to tell us why it is so difficult to get this precious liquid for our children. This man who reignited the hopes of
many of my compatriots must now come forward and express himself; confess his failure or at least explain why he
failed.

I am waiting for a clarification about why Obama's proposal for US telecommunications companies to provide
Internet to the Cuban people wasn't accepted. I demand,
along with many others, a convincing argument about why
we are not going to join the OAS, and the reasons for still
not implementing the International Covenant on Economic, Social and Cultural Rights and the International
Covenant on Civil and Political Rights.

The list of unanswered questions is long, and to hide
from so many questions is not going to solve the problems.
Please, let somebody—with answers—come forward soon.

The extinction of the Panda

The last domestic appliance distributed through the merit
system was a Chinese Panda brand television. In my building there was a meeting to distribute ten new Pandas
among more than three hundred people, at the price of
four thousand Cuban pesos. Some neighbors nearly came
to blows during the meeting. Among those who took home
the color TVs were, coincidentally, the most combative and
ideologically unyielding.

Those who didn't catch the elusive Panda consoled themselves by thinking that there would be a second round and they'd have a better chance. But the Asian giant didn't send any new televisions, nor even spare parts to fix the existing ones. Serving on the Committee for the Defense of the Revolution (CDR) and going to the "criticism meetings" suddenly lost their appeal. It appeared that there would no longer be any reward in the form of a washing machine, a telephone line, or a portable radio.

People who won the last round of appliance allocations aren't very happy either. Many haven't been able to meet the payment deadlines, because the Panda monthly installment equals a third of their salary. I know one elderly woman who bought the fought-over television only because she was convinced she would die before she finished paying for it.

Those who thought of the allocation as a benefit now worry about the enormous debt they've contracted with the State.

Yes I want

Last week I participated in a Web literacy program for those new to blogging. After six months of our Blogger Journey meetings, we found we needed to start separate sessions for people taking their first steps into the blogosphere. Like teaching someone to spell, these classes teach participants the basics of joining texts and images and how to upload posts.

We teach them how to use Wordpress. Our teaching

philosophy is something we call "Yes I want," because the desire to express one's personal opinions is the guiding principle. Teachers are giving each student a pair of wings, but it is up to the students to decide if they want to fly. We show them how to express themselves in cyberspace—without asking for any kind of commitment or loyalty.

"Yes I want"—because the pull of desire can lead us to do what not even our willpower can accomplish. When you've grown up surrounded by slogans, your behavior mandated, expressing your personal desires is a form of victory. "Yes I want" should accompany the oft-mentioned, "Yes I can." The capacity to learn is not enough if we lack the appetite to use this learning about posts and kilobytes to fly.

Caught in the wave

I missed the controversial German film *The Wave* during the German Film Festival. I managed to rent a copy via the underground distribution network, however, and watched it at home with some friends. Our debate continues because there was so much in it that resembles our own experience.

I recognize many characteristics of an autocracy. I, too, was a uniformed Pioneer. I was glad because I only had one change of clothes—the red skirt and white blouse of the school uniform. Every day I repeated that gesture which, compared with the salute in *The Wave*, seems like child's play. Fingers united and hand tensed at the temple, I saluted, promising to be like an Argentinean who'd died fifteen years earlier. That military salute was pointed at my head like a weapon, a kind of self-threat I was forced to perform along with the slogan, "Pioneers for communism, we will be like Che."

I also believed I had been born on a chosen island, under a superior social system, guided by the best possible leaders. Those who ruled us weren't "Aryan," but they were self-titled "revolutionaries" and this seemed to be a more evolved state—the highest rung—of human development. I learned to march. I dragged myself to interminable classes on military preparation and knew how to use an AK-47 before I was fifteen. Meanwhile, with the nationalistic slogans we shouted, we tried to hide our dependence on the East, and my friends' ongoing emigration.

But our autocracy produced unexpected results, far from fanaticism or veneration. Instead of stern-faced soldiers, it bred apathy, indifference, people who concealed their true selves, rafters, infidels, and young people fascinated by material goods. It also produced packs of zealots who formed the Rapid Response Brigades.[22]

The belief that one belonged to a society that was a shining example to the world faded like the false essence of cheap perfume. Nevertheless, the autocrats remained. My teacher, Professor Wenger, continued to stand in front of the class shouting and demanding that we get up from our chairs, over and over.

Ours is not a weeklong experiment with a few students in a classroom. We are caught in *The Wave*, swallowed and drowned by it, without ever being able to touch bottom.

Culture for the chosen

We were planning to celebrate Reinaldo's birthday at Pedro Luís Ferrar's "Velorio" concert at the Museum of Decorative Arts in Vedado. But, using their bodies like barricades, the culture police wouldn't let us enter.

They accused us of planning a major provocation at the concert, even though, for us, it was they and the state television cameras they'd called out that caused all the commotion. I think the "restless boys" of State Security have been watching too many late-night movies. Our plans weren't that unusual—we even took our son with us. We were going to listen to the songs of the well-known musician and then drop by a friend's house.

But, at the Museum entry a real repudiation meeting-was waiting for us, all it lacked was eggs and blows.[23] One man, who would not identify himself, yelled at me "you want to destroy Cuban culture," adding that this space was "only for the People." It seems that Tania Bruguera's performance rubbed bureaucrats the wrong way. They feared we'd planned to seize the microphones—as if it wouldn't be better to put a loudspeaker on every corner for anyone who has something to say.

Many who were there and saw this abuse of institutional power avoided us, knowing they were being watched by the huge force that had surrounded the place. But others, whose names I withhold to protect them, did show solidarity and weren't afraid to be seen with us.

We stayed outside, while inside a strange audience of retirees and men with military haircuts silently listened to Pedro Luís sing, seemingly for the first time. Some friends, among them Claudia, came out to show solidarity with our enforced "exile," and we stayed until the last chord was played. When all the musical instruments were packed up, the singer came out and expressed surprise over what had happened. He said he would speak to the vice-minister about it. We didn't want to discourage him, but I don't think that official could do anything to restrain the repressive body whose actions were on view today, a body of which, perhaps, he is a part.

Since I know they read my blog—all those who prevented me from entering seemed to know me—I want to tell them that they are not going to force me to withdraw into my house. I won't stop going to concerts, clubs, cultural or comedy events. I'm a cultured person, even though they want to reserve that designation for the ideologically-screened chosen ones. They will have to stand guard at the doors of every theater, club, and music room. I could show up at any of them. And who knows if I might climb onto the dais and take the microphone?

Social workers: the ephemeral body of action

They appeared in my neighborhood one day, in their red shirts, to inventory old American refrigerators and Soviet air conditioners. They came fully vested with the power of the State. Early one morning they even descended on service stations to stop the illegal sale of petrol. They were young people who hadn't been able to enroll in a university. And a plan—made at the highest levels—converted them into an army ready for any task, by promising them all a slot in some form of higher education.

Given a new set of clothes, flamboyant and imposing, they moved across the country in brand-new Chinese buses. They were authorized to appear at any labor center and ask for accounts, do an audit, and even replace personnel, earning the alarming nickname, "Children of the *Comandante*."

They changed light bulbs on the streets of Caracas, and they watched over salespeople in the convertible-peso stores. They were the new eyes of power among us, and they came from the generation most affected by the Special Period, the dual monetary system, and the fading of a myth. So, it was not uncommon to see them exchange their self-confidence for obedience and their bright slogans for listless phrases. Their brilliance was as brief as the crispness of the blue jeans they were allocated when they started out.

Some of them abandoned their ten-year commitment, though leaving was difficult and resulted in a black mark on their file. Today, one hardly hears about them. Although there was no announcement that they are demobilized, their work certainly lacks substance. Now, there are no electric pots to distribute, no public-opinion surveys to conduct. The enormous physical infrastructure of shelters, snacks, and buses that supported their work is no longer guaranteed. I rarely run into any of them on the street. Those I do see no longer have that arrogant air, that apparent sense of belonging to an elite.

Chicken for fish

Saturday morning, I heard that chicken had arrived at

the ration market. I went to the butcher shop, where they usually sell eggs and soy-based "ground meat." But there weren't any customers. The employee mutely pointed a finger, calling my attention to the hundred people in line in front of the fish store.

For some time there's been a seafood shortage. The natural source of phosphorus was more elusive than buried treasure. Marked in the ration book where there should be a note for a portion of mackerel or hake, they now enter a tiny portion of thigh, and next to "thigh," the word "chicken." I spent two hours waiting and finally entered the place, where nothing remained but the odor of the African coasts, which is where the fishing fleet captures its fish... in this time of true socialism.

The seller was standing on a mat made of cartons where one could read—perfectly clearly—the origin of the merchandise: "Made in USA." An old man with a malicious tongue didn't miss this detail and commented, "These American chickens are certainly well fed." The lady took our ration book, which specifies that we are three people, and threw thirty-three ounces on the scale, none of which was breast, telling me the price was one peso fifty centavos. "When is the fish coming?" I inquired. She didn't answer me but instead pointed an index finger at the sky.

Overstepping the boundaries

Seven months after they warned me, in a dark police station, "You have transgressed all limits of tolerance," I continue to travel to Pinar del Río to conduct our Blogger Journey classes. Instead of curing the virus of expressing ourselves online, that December ban on our meeting has fueled, in many, the desire to become infected.

Adiós to schools in the countryside

The idea of combining agricultural labor and high school looked good on paper. It had an air of a glorious future about it, in whatever ministerial office came up with the idea. But reality, stubborn as always, had its own interpretation of schools in the countryside. The "clay" meant to be molded by love of the furrow was made up of adolescents far from parental control—many for the first time—who found the housing conditions and food very different from their expectations.

I, who was to be this "New Man," was trained in one of these schools in the municipality of Alquizar. I was fourteen, and by the time I returned home I had a corneal infection, a liver deficiency and the toughness acquired when one has seen too much. On entering the school, I still believed the fairy-tales about work-study; on leaving, I knew that many of my fellow students had had to exchange sex for good grades or high marks in agricultural production. Whether it was the lettuce beds I weeded every afternoon or the hostel where bullying and lack of respect for privacy ruled, the harsh law of survival-of-the-fittest reigned.

And it was on one of those afternoons—after three days with no water supply and with the same menu of rice and cabbage—that I promised myself that my children would never go to a high school in the countryside. I did this with an unsentimental adolescent realism that calmed me at the time, but that also left me knowing that some promises will never be kept.

So, I got used to making up bags of food for Teo when he was away at school, of hearing that they stole his shoes, or threatened him in the shower, or that one of the bigger boys took his food.

Fortunately, the experiment seems to be ending. Lack of productivity, spread of disease, damage to morals, and low academic standards have discredited this education method. After years of financial losses, with students consuming more than they manage to extract from the land, our authorities have decided that the best place for a young person is at his parents' side. They announced the coming closings without a trace of a public apology to those of us who were guinea pigs for this failed experiment, to those of us who left our dreams and our health in the countryside.

Milk, water, and shadow

July 26, 2009: Raúl Castro's words on July 26, 2007 were christened by the population "the milk speech" because of his call to increase dairy production.[24] In the next speech, which he made a year later, he aimed lower and only promised to solve the water problems of the province of Santiago de Cuba. Everything seems to indicate that his address this past Sunday will be remembered for its beginning, where he referred to the fact that he was backlit by the sun: "I'm sure that none of you can see me; you will see, perhaps, a shadow: That's me."

The general made no notable pronouncements, nor did he allude to the olive branch he had said he was willing to extend to the American administration. Nor did he detail any future projects or measures for ending the crisis, much less confirm whether the Communist Party Sixth Congress will be held at all. He limited himself to informing us about upcoming meetings of government bodies where, it seems, some decisions will be made. The Holguín sun found the plaza full of white and red T-shirts, presided over by an ancient orator without much to say. The applause lacked enthusiasm, and, even watching it on TV, I could see the shared desire for it to be over, as soon as possible.

On returning home, thousands who were present will have little to report. It wasn't a trick of the sunlight that made a shadow of someone who has never shone with his own spark. This was the speech of the "shadow." Light is something authoritarians cannot tame, something that disobeys military uniforms. Raúl Castro is right: We can no longer see him. The twilight he represents lacks, as it has for a long time, any kind of luminosity.

Maria Moors Cabot

Years ago I turned my back on academia and the intellectual world. I was tired of seeing only masks covering the faces of my teachers and fellow students. Today begins my journey back to the university campus, with the help of a special citation in the Maria Moors Cabot Journalism prizes, awarded by Columbia University. A prize that I've received, in part, for refusal to take part in the "cultivated" complicity that so frustrated me in Cuban academe.

Escaping from a bookish detachment from reality, I went to the opposite extreme: to circuitry and binary code. There are roads, however, that always lead to the same place, and that can make a renegade philologist re-embrace the habits of the academy—particularly if this return is for having behaved as a free person in cyberspace.

I hope I can use the prestige and protection of the Cabot Prize to continue to grow the Cuban blogosphere. The alternative Blogger Journey that unites us every week has reached a point where it must become an authentic blogger academy. As I don't plan to wait for permission to open a school of digital journalism, I consider this a formal statement of its inauguration. The distinction that I have received today can contribute to the birth of a new kind of instruction, one without ideological conditions, and without the masks which made me distance myself from the academic world.

When I am pessimistic

There is no way to look at my son and not predict that in a few years he will be climbing aboard a raft to go to Florida or be married to a foreigner and intending to leave Cuba. Just looking at him I realize that he will, at all costs, try to leave behind this piece of land, tied as he is by the stubbornness of his parents and the bureaucratic absurdity that prevents him from traveling. Though he hardly knows it, today he is a fledgling who some day will spread his wings and fly. An embryonic exile, awaiting for his destination.

I would love nothing more than if he would stay. But I don't have a single convincing argument to offer him. What reason could I give for staying? What optimistic predictions would be enough? Will there be any hints of change here to make him abandon his idea? If I myself am not sure he should stay here, how could I tell him to put down roots in a country where so few bear fruit?

After Raúl Castro's speech before the National Assembly, with its "shadow" of continuity, and its aura of "more of the same," with its dull oratory of times gone by, I only have the urge to be—for my son—his oar, sail, visa, wing... on the road to his early escape.

Adiós, muchachos, "compañeros" of my life...

There are words that have their moment, while others manage to survive and remain in our everyday lives. The longevity of some words contrasts with the brief lives of others, condemned to oblivion and mentioned only to evoke the past. We choose among these words every day. Hence, the public death of a politician starts when people cease to create nicknames for him; an ideal's crisis appears when few make reference to it, and ideological propaganda falters when no one repeats the slogans. Language can validate or bury any utopia.

Among the linguistic evidence of our lack of appetite for the current regime is the gradual disappearance of the term "compañero." This formula is used less and less to refer to a lifelong friend or to someone we meet for the first time. Having banished—for their petit-bourgeois inferences—the titles "señor," "señora" and "señorita," we came up with others, such as the imported "comrade," to suggest a greater familiarity among Cubans. They were even used in tragicomic circumstances—such as when a person referred to a certain bureaucrat, who had made her wait six hours for a form, as "compañero," even though what she really wanted to do was insult him.

For years, unless you addressed someone as "compañero," as prescribed by the Party, you could be seen as ideologically deviant. We were all "equal." Even the use of the formal form of "you" disappeared in this false familiarity that often degenerated into disrespect. On opening the island to tourism, one of the first lessons the hotel employees learned was to use the stigmatized "señor" when dealing with guests. Little by little, titles of the recent past were reduced to the vocabulary of the most loyal, the oldest. So, among the thousands of salutations you hear today on our streets—dude, bro, pal, buddy, friend, man, or just "pssst"—the sonorous syllables of "compañero" are heard less and less.

Antihero

He could have been an alcoholic lying on a street corner sleeping it off, like so many others in this city, but he also wanted to act. He jumped in front of the camera and cried for food, which, along with a yearning for change, has become a national obsession. His spontaneity, and his cry for "grub" turned the brief video of Juan Carlos, alias *Pánfilo* or Dimwit, into a "superhit" on the alternative information networks. I don't remember anything going viral this quickly, not even last year's video of the student Eliécer Ávila versus vice president Ricardo Alarcón.

Pánfilo knew a few days after the broadcast that he had been denounced. His words were like a red circle around his head, a neon sign in front of his house, a finger pointed at his life. The magnifying glass of power, which hangs over us all, focused on him and began to rummage through his weaknesses. Managing to stay afloat with no work, he had been prosecuted for theft; he had probably bought rum on the black market and committed many of the other outrages we Cubans engage in every day to survive or escape. It was enough that he was sincere in front of the cameras and took off his mask, to feel the scalpel of repression slicing through his life.

In a society where punishment awaits those who express opinions, neither fools nor children say what they think, only drunkards. So I wasn't surprised when that they found Pánfilo to be a criminal, charged him with "precriminal dangerousness," and gave him two years in prison. The judicial process must have sobered him up faster than a bucket of cold water and a cup of strong coffee. Although it's still possible to appeal the decision, it's unlikely that he'll get off without punishment. It is a lesson aimed not only at him. If they don't condemn him, what will prevent other neighborhood drunks from standing up in front of a camera and shouting for everything we lack: Food! Future! Freedom!

Bulletin boards

The paper was recently stuck on a wall in Tulipan Street: "I unblock cell phones," it said, and gave the phone number of the shrewd technician. More and more frequently, you see ads offering puppies for sale, auto parts, or the services of someone who repairs kitchens or polishes floors. They're put up by the most daring in the informal market for services, trades and offerings that we all depend on.

These little handwritten cards remind me of the workplaces and schools outside Cuba where I was fascinated by the bulletin boards crammed with requests and offers. "Cheap lodging," "I want to buy a laptop," or a trip that needs "new riders to help pay for the transport," were some of the classifieds I saw posted. None of this can be read on the boring walls, covered with political slogans, that appear in Cuban universities, factories, and businesses. Students and workers are not authorized to have a physical space to post a little paper asking for a book, a computer part, or a room to rent. Nor are there any websites or local radio or television channels willing to devote a few minutes to swaps or lost objects.

To me, not allowing bulletin boards is one of the most visible signs that all kinds of spontaneous organization and interactions among citizens are controlled. These boards stuffed with ads energize a city and give life to schools, offices and shops. But here, posting the smallest card to sell X or buy Y is an act of transgression, something you must only do at night, in the shadows, when no one is looking.

So little birdseed for such a large cage

Speculation grows about the disappearance of food rationing. Amid fear and hope, some say that by early 2010 the
quota for salt and sugar will already be history and that lib-
eralization of other foods will follow. Those who are frightened by this can't imagine a life without benefits from the
State, without the crutch of subsidization. I myself was
born entered into a ration book where every gram of what I
put into my mouth was written down. Had I grown up only
on what was regulated, I would have a body even more rickety than the one I now possess. Fortunately, life has many
more options than the grids on which, every month, the
shopkeeper marks the minimal rations received.

If the 66 million pounds of rice rationed every month
were available via a free market, prices would go down. You
could decide, instead of buying rice again, to buy potatoes
or vegetables. And no one would declare, "I will take everything they give me, before I will leave it in the shop."
And there wouldn't be that feeling that they are giving us
something—especially that sense of guilt that keeps us
from protesting or criticizing those who guarantee these
tiny portions. The ration market should remain for those
who suffer physical or psychological impairment or who are
unemployed. In short, it should go to those who need social
security to survive.

Although the idea seems simple, the stumbling block is
that wages are adjusted to subsidized food prices and don't
relate to free prices. To say to a Cuban family that starting
tomorrow they will not receive the limited quantities and
doubtful quality they currently get from the ration store,

would be to saw off the one branch on which they're standing. The birdseed is difficult to eliminate because you can
only get rid of it once you open the cage doors.

So, the real news we are waiting for is not the end of rationing, but rather the end of economic handicaps, the end
of the paternalistic relationship that keeps us like pigeons,
dependent and... hungry.

Bluetooth: to say without words

They were three meters from each other and pointed their
mobile phones—like two cowboys in the middle of a duel—
to send the video clip "Decadence" and the latest photos
of Carlos Lage. The information traveled through the air
and stored itself in the memory of each telephone device. It
left no traces of the shipment, not even those around them
realized that almost fifty megabytes had crossed the park
in a few short minutes. As the night advanced, they passed
the "materials" to a dozen friends, who transferred it to
another fifty.

Bluetooth technology is the nightmare of the censors.
Prohibited books, songs you'll never hear on the radio, blogs
blocked inside the Island, and every kind of news missing
from the official media is transmitted through these radio
frequencies. In the capital, it is a growing phenomenon,
especially among the young. Some carry a cellphone used
only to store and share photos, music, and videos, because
they can't afford the high price of mobile service.

The intangible is making its way, in a place where printing and distributing a publication can lead to prison for

disseminating "enemy propaganda." Many exclusively virtual newspapers are seeing the light of day. Digital culture
is leaving out in the cold those who think revolutions are
made of weapons and speeches. For them, these omnidirec-
tional waves are pure child's play. It is better that they think
so. By the time they realize their importance, wireless will
have managed to reconnect all these threads that have been
cut, systematically, between citizens.

A sanatorium for Pánfilo ... and food? And freedom?

I woke to news of Pánfilo being transferred from prison to
a psychiatric clinic, perhaps to start his detox. On the list
of victories won for Cuban civil society over the last year—
which are still few and limited—we can add the release of
this humble man from his cell. On the short list of accomplishments should also be the freeing of Gorki Aguila over
a year ago and the decision not to enforce a resolution preventing Cubans from connecting to the Internet in hotels.

I think what happened in the case of "Pánfilo" has been
the work of the campaign Food and Freedom, which just
yesterday presented three thousand signatures calling for
his release. We must also thank the international media
that helped call attention to the unjust two-year sentence.
The alternative blogosphere—as expected—helped push
the wall, which seemed to grow stronger on that day when
they imprisoned someone who was merely demanding
food.

In any case, the blunder of charging an inoffensive
neighborhood drunk with "pre-criminal dangerousness"

won't easily be forgotten. Now we hope that he can return home and have access to the food every human being deserves and the freedom of expression to say what he wants without being hauled in front of a prosecutor. For those who have been debating the pros and cons of Columbian superstar Juanes's upcoming "Concert for Peace" in the Plaza of the Revolution, his attention to the campaign to free Pánfilo seems to have borne fruit, which is one more reason to applaud the concert. It's too bad we have to wait for the famous to visit Cuba to pull back the bolts, but regardless of this detail, we count the triumph as our own.

Veiled confession

"It will be resolved in another way," Jorge told his brother when he learned that lunch would be abolished in several workplaces. His salary as a cook in a state agency has him living on the margins, but thanks to selling food on the black market, he's managed to exchange his small house for a bigger one. He acquired a DVD player that allows him to avoid the boring State television programming, and he has even taken his kids on vacation to Varadero. His own business was simple: He provided rice to a kiosk that offered boxed lunches, he supplied oil to another entrepreneur, and a sandwich seller paid him for bread that never quite made it to lunch trays.

Now, everything seems to be over for Jorge. Several ministries will distribute fifteen Cuban pesos to their employees for lunch. The amount has surprised many—especially those who earn less than that for an eight-hour work day. If the Cuban government is acknowledging that fifteen pesos is the amount needed to cover the cost of lunch, then they are also acknowledging that they need to pay at least three times this amount for each day of work.

Now Jorge is thinking about taking on a new position at his company. Until a week ago, this particular job had too many responsibilities and not enough perks, but suddenly it has become an attractive post. He would be confirming how many days each employee works and is entitled to the new lunch payment. He is already planning on taking a broad view toward absences and sharing the lunch money with the employees. He will happily exchange sacks of beans and flour for names and punch cards. Maybe next year he'll be able to take his family to Baracoa beach.

The flight of the Suzuki over Taguayabón

The indigenous name and broken bridge contribute to the feeling that Taguayabón is a town stranded in the early twenthieth century. So it seemed to me, anyway, when three weeks ago we infected Villa Clara province with the blogger virus. The amazed eyes of those who had never seen the Web looked through the copies of the blogs we had brought. Explaining Google to them was complicated. In Cuba, a simple search in the civic registry for a birth certificate is extremely difficult. Imagine the surprise when they discovered that, with one simple click, they can see a list of all the references to a fact, a personality, or particular subject matter.

Reinaldo and I talked with about a dozen people about

citizens' access to new technology. When we left to visit another area, a flight of motorcycles—Suzukis, the preferred transport for State Security—glided along the small main street and the parallel routes. Several participants from that day were interrogated—which intimidated the youngest. They even confiscated a horse which—I can assure you—had nothing to do with the Blogger Journey. The fear they spread strangled the virtual breath of air that had briefly wafted over the inhabitants of Villa Clara. The "restless boys" who remain in the shadows returned to repeat the same old same old: The CIA and the Pentagon are behind the alternative Cuban blogosphere, they said. But the virus of Wordpress and Blogger had already spread. Tuesday, some inhabitants of Taguayabón called to say, "We want to start publishing on the Internet."

Pandemic and detergent

I search, without success, for a bottle of detergent to wash glasses smeared with grease and fingerprints. Looking for the soapy liquid, I walked a good part of Havana today, as television announcers call on us to redouble our hygiene efforts before the advance of the H1N1 virus. The alert has not caused shops to lower the price of cleaning products, not even the cost of simple soap, the equivalent of a full day's wages. Instead, the opposite has happened. The collapse in imports affects these products most.

The announcer says to wash our hands often, use handkerchiefs when we sneeze, and maintain good personal hygiene, but the reality forces us into filth. We lack face masks, running water in many houses, the simple possession of vitamin C to strengthen the immune system, and cleanliness in public places. Thus, the so-called "swine flu" has fertile ground to reproduce. It advances through our neighborhoods, and the official media don't mention the closed schools, the quarantined sites, and the full hospitals.

This illusion of paradise is killing us. We cannot hide the fragility of our society in the face of an epidemic that requires material resources in the hands of citizens. If soaping the body and having a bit of alcohol to sterilize the hands become luxuries, how can we stop the pandemic that is already upon us? If the September supply of soap never even reached the ration stores, how is it possible that they call for hygiene? Is it that they haven't noticed that we are sinking into the dirt? They have to face the ravages of conjunctivitis, diarrhea, and viruses to figure out that sanitation is not just about a white coat and a stethoscope. It starts in the streets, with collecting the garbage, with showers in the homes, and with a mother who can wash the plate her child eats from.

I had a neckerchief; so what?

Across the country, today, October 8, is the ceremony for first-grade students to enroll in the Pioneers. The morning assembly lasts longer than usual and parents accompany their children while they put on the neckerchiefs and shout, for the first time, "Pioneers for communism, we will be like Che!" I went through this twice, my own ceremony and my son Teo's. My recollections of the two are so different that they seem to have occurred in diametrically opposed dimensions.

In my case it was during years of ideological fervor, and barely three feet tall, I was determined to give my life for that blue neckerchief. I felt touched by the hand of the Fatherland, though in reality I was only being inscribed into the ranks of an ideology. The shouted slogan seemed like magic words that would open all doors to me; only much later would I learn that the suffix "ism" forms nouns meaning "doctrine, sect, system." Nor did I want to be like Lybna, a Jehovah's Witness, who did not take "her vows" with the rest of us. A dark cloud hovered around her because the blue cloth was not tied around her neck.

Twenty years passed, and I was there with my son on an October morning to see him initiated into a movement in which I no longer believed. The teacher walked up and down the ranks and asked the children to repeat the slogan about Che Guevara. Teo remained silent, and his pout didn't escape the eagle eyes of the principal. When she asked him why he didn't say the slogan he pointed out, with childish simplicity, "Because Che is dead and I don't want to be dead."

I assumed that my son was about to be logged into the ideological catalog under the worst letter, the "C" for "counterrevolutionary." But no, the teacher laughed and gave him his first lesson in opportunism, "Ah Teo, repeat the slogan, why make problems for yourself."

Architecture of the emergency

In the early morning they removed the first bricks from

the exterior wall to sell at three pesos—each—on the black market. Like an army of ants, the poorest people in the area began to dismantle the old factory. Some kids served as lookouts in case the police came, while their parents sifted through debris to extract mortar. Deft hands knocked it down during the day and carried it away at night—construction materials for their own homes. After three weeks, all that was left of the enormous building was its floor and some columns, standing in a vacuum. Everything that could be used had been moved, gone to support the architecture of the emergency.

On this Island where acquiring cement, blocks, or steel is comparable to getting a bit of lunar dust, destroying in order to build has become common practice. There are specialists in extracting clay bricks intact, experts in peeling off tiles, and adroit "deconstructors" who extract metal girders from the collapsed heaps. They use the reclaimed materials to build their own habitable spaces because no one can legally buy a house. Their main "quarries" are those houses that have collapsed or workplaces abandoned by an apathetic State. They fall on them with an efficiency that one might like to see in the dozing bricklayers who work for wages.

Some of these skilled recyclers have been killed by a collapsing roof or a falling wall. But sometimes Lady Luck smiles and they find a toilet without cracks, or an electric socket that owners of the demolished house didn't take with them. A small dwelling of tin and zinc a few kilometers from the looting site begins to change. The tiled floor from a house at Neptuno and Aguila streets has been added, along with a piece of the exterior railing from an abandoned mansion on Linea Street, and even some stained glass from a convent in Old Havana. Inside this house, the fruit of pillaging, a family—equally plundered by life—dreams of the next building that will be dismantled and loaded onto its shoulders.

The notes of the new anthem

"How do you shout on Twitter?" That was one of the first messages I sent to explore the potential of one hundred and forty characters.

Today, October 19, 2009, I ask: How do you sing the anthem of a people mobilized on the Internet, how do you broadcast the desire for change that I see in everyone around me? Before, it was the sound of bugles, galloping horses, and stanzas that summoned the citizens of Bayamo to "die for the Fatherland"; now everything is different.[25]

It occurs to me to take advantage of the cutting edge of this new world, sharper than a machete, to slaughter authoritarianism and censorship. To launch a call for:

- Freedom of opinion
- Freedom of access to the Internet
- Freedom to enter and leave Cuba
- Freedom of association
- Freedom for prisoners of conscience
- Freedom for Cuba

What they promised us

I was ten in my red-and-white uniform. The subject of the "blockade" was barely mentioned in my ideology-filled school books. Those were optimistic times, and we believed that the F1 cows would give so much milk it would flood the streets.[26] The future had golden hues matching nothing in our faded reality, but we were a too colorblind to notice. We thought we had discovered the formula to be among the most prosperous people on the planet, that our children would live in a country with opportunities for all.

From the podium a bearded leader defiantly pointed to the North, counting on the pole of the Kremlin subsidy to vault over any obstacle to the construction of communism. "Despite the blockade..." we said, with the same conviction that in years past we'd talked about the ten million tons of sugar, coffee growing around the cities, and a supposed industrialization of the country that never came.[27] When the flow of oil and rubles abruptly stopped, our dreams were cut short. Then came excuses for the setbacks, and comparisons to the poorest nations in the region to make us feel, if not happy, at least satisfied.

As I began my adolescence, the issue of trade restrictions was on nearly every billboard in the country. At political rallies we no longer shouted, "Cuba yes! Yankees no!" but a new hard-to-rhyme slogan: "Down with the blockade." I looked at my nearly empty plate and couldn't imagine how they had managed to blockade our malangas, orange juice, bananas, and lemons. I grew up repudiating the blockade because we were told it was the reason for all our problems.

If my friends were leaving the country, it was because

of the United States policy of harassment; if cockroaches were crawling all over the walls at the maternity hospital, it was the fault of North Americans; if the university expelled a critical colleague, it was because he had fallen under the ideological influence of the enemy. Today, everything begins and ends with the blockade. No one seems to remember the days when they promised us paradise, when they told us that nothing—not even the economic sanctions—would prevent us from leaving behind our underdevelopment.

In my absence and with love

I can't remember the last time I cried, even though I'm not particularly strong in the face of life's vagaries. Actually, I consider myself overly sentimental and given to tears. However, for over a year now I've decided to be happy at any cost, to inoculate myself with placidity because I anticipate worse times. I resist letting my smile dim, or becoming paranoid, and refuse to always be looking over my shoulder to see who is following me.

My childish inclination to play has allowed me to cope with the denial of permission to travel, the radioactive circle they've drawn around me, the insults, the defamation campaigns, the political police, and even the paranoia about possible microphones in my house. I have tried to celebrate even what's been taken from me: The possibility to travel; attending the award ceremonies for prizes I have won; accessing my blog from Cuban networks; maintaining contact with many of my friends; attending cultural events in my own country; and being present at the launch of my books.

Today, Octobert 29, I am drunk with happiness because a Portuguese edition of my book, entitled *De Cuba, com carinho (From Cuba with Love)*, is being launched this afternoon in Brazil. Because of the three-hour time difference between here and Rio de Janeiro, at precisely 5:00 pm I will celebrate the beautiful new edition. My gap-toothed grin will be visible from yards away—a purifying laugh that the grim ones who have prevented me from going cannot understand; a stab of delight that cuts and pierces those who don't know how to handle the unexpected joy of the captive.

Closed doors

Where to begin to tell about what happened in the debate about the Internet organized by the magazine *Temas* yesterday, October 29? The blond wig I wore allowed me to slip through the guarded entrance of the Fresa y Chocolate Cultural Center. That and high heels, lipstick, shiny earrings and an enormous, painfully bright purse transformed me into someone sufficiently different. Some friends told me that I looked better like that—with a tight-fitting short dress, a sexy walk, and square-framed glasses. My apologies to them—the act didn't last long, and today I've returned to my disheveled and boring appearance.

Claudia, Reinaldo, Eugenio, Ciro, and other bloggers were not allowed to enter. "The institution reserves the right of admission," they were told. Already excluded from other places, my colleagues showed their impertinence by not retreating in embarrassed silence. Inside, I managed to find a seat next to the panel of speakers. Some sharp eyes detected my reedy physiognomy and a camera filmed me continuously, as though preparing a dossier.

A young writer asked to speak and bemoaned the fact that so many were denied entrance. Then someone replied, using words such as "enemy," "dangerous," and "defend ourselves." When I finally was called on, I asked what relationship exists between limitations in bandwidth and the many websites censored for the Cuban public. There was applause when I finished. I swear I didn't arrange that with anyone. Afterward, a university professor questioned my receiving the Ortega y Gasset journalism prize. I still haven't managed to discover the connection between my question and her response, but the paths of defamation are twisted. At the end, several people came up and hugged me, one woman just tapped me and said "Congratulations." The crisp October night waited outside.

If everyone who was denied participation had been there, it would have been a true space for debate about the Web. But it felt withered and shackled. Only one of the speakers mentioned things such as Web 2.0, social networks, and Wikipedia. The rest was the usual defense against the perversities of the Web, repeated justifications for why all Cubans cannot access it. I quickly Tweeted, "I think it would be best to organize another debate about the Internet, without the burden of censorship and exclusion." This morning, with dark circles under my eyes from only three hours of sleep, I was handing out technical manuals in the second session of our Blogger Academy.

[Note: From a transcript generously prepared by two of the

*readers of the blog. The event was clandestinely videotaped by
some participants.]*

[Yoani goes to the microphone]

VOICE FROM AUDIENCE: They do damage to Cuban-ness,
they do damage to the Fatherland, they do damage not only
to our Fatherland.......

YOANI: Well, I'm glad my name has been mentioned, I have
come incognito, but I'm happy to be here. No, no, I know,
but I would like to ask.... What relationship exists between
bandwidth, the trumpeted bandwidth that every now and
then they bring up to explain why we Cuban citizens cannot access the Internet en masse, and the censored sites?

I'm talking about a variety of sites where one may find
things as inoffensive as a parish in the Canary Islands where
Cubans can find the birth certificates of our grandparents.
A site like Cuba Encuentro, Cuba Net, Voces Cubanas, a
magnificent blogger platform that is maintained from
Cuba, but which was censored as of the last week of August.
My own website that has existed for more than a year and
a half. This is the same ideological screening that was used
to exclude from this debate people like Claudia Cadelo from
the *Octavo Cerco* blog, a magnificent window open to the
real Cuba, to the Cuba of a generation that has never spo-
ken out. Blogs like *Desde Aqui*, by a journalist expelled from
the official media, my husband Reinaldo Escobar.

That is also why I have come here, in this way, having
outflanked the police surrounding my home to come to

this debate. Why in the virtual Cuba is censorship being repeated, intimidation, stigmatization of people because they think differently? Is this "cyber-garbage"? Is writing what you call "garbage" the same as telling the truth without subterfuge? Is writing what you call "garbage" the same as not bowing before an official opinion? I was born in a tenement in Central Havana in the Cayo Hueso neighborhood. If what we say is "cyber-garbage," let it be welcomed. This society needs it.

A question of tones

"I stopped for you because you're white," the taxi driver tells me after his tires peel out into Reina Street around midnight. From wide mulatto lips come the justifications, one after another, for why he doesn't accept clients "of color" at this late hour. He looks for complicity in me, born in a mostly black neighborhood and a lover of cinnamon-colored skin. I barely listen to him. Those who discriminate against people like themselves especially bother me: the hotel doorman who berates the Cuban but lets a wildly shouting tourist pass; the prostitute who will go, for ten convertible pesos, with a Canadian twice her age but doesn't want to seem "defeated" by accepting a fellow Cuban; the Santiaguan who, once living in Havana, mocks the accents of people from his own city.

I often wish I was mixed, like Reinaldo and Teo, because when you look at my straight nose and pale skin you think I have it easy. But it's not true. There are many ways of being ostracized. Along with racism, here we have discrimination based on social origin, the stigma of ideological affiliation, and exclusion for not belonging to a family clan with power, influence, or relationships. Not to mention how you are patronized in a macho society if you have a pair of ovaries hidden in the middle of your belly.

And so I am bothered by the driver's dissertation on how he stopped the car because of the pallor of my skin. I want to get out, but it's late, very late.

"What do you do?" he asks me under the streetlights of Belascoain Street. I'm a blogger, I warn him, and the lights of Carlos III Avenue show me his suspicious and fearful face. "Look, don't go and tell what I just said," he says, changing the indulgent tone he used when picking me up. "I don't want you to publish some nonsense about me on the Internet," he clarifies, while grabbing his crotch in a gesture of power. My straight hair is no longer a reason to trust me, now my eyes don't seem so almond-shaped. When I explain—through narrow lips—the subjects I deal with on my blog, it's as if I am threatening him, razor in hand, a dangerous criminal. So, I confirm that his classification system stigmatizes not only based on skin tones, but also by certain opinions, those invisible tones that on this Island also lead to segregation and rejection.

A gangland-style kidnapping

Near 23rd Street, we saw a black Chinese-make car pull up with three heavily built strangers. "Yoani, get in the car," one told me, grabbing my wrist. The other two surrounded Claudia Cadelo, Orlando Luis Pardo Lazo, and a friend who was accompanying us to the march against violence. It was an evening of punches, shouts, and obscenities on what should have been a day of peace and harmony. The "aggressors" called for a patrol car to take two of my companions, while Orlando and I were forced into the car with yellow plates, the terrifying world of lawlessness with the impunity of Armageddon.

I refused to get into the car and demanded that they show us identification or a warrant, but they refused to show us any papers to prove the legitimacy of our arrest. To curious onlookers crowded around I shouted, "Help, these men want to kidnap us!" but those who tried to intervene were stopped with a shout that revealed the whole ideological background of the operation, "Don't mess with it, these are counterrevolutionaries!"

In response to our verbal resistance they made a phone call to ask someone who must have been the boss, "What do we do? They don't want to get in the car." I imagine the answer from the other side was unequivocal, because then with a flurry of punches and pushes, they pushed my head down to force me into the car. I held onto the door... blows to my knuckles... I managed to grab a paper one of them had in his pocket and put it in my mouth. Another flurry of punches so I would return the document to them.

Orlando was already inside, with his head to the floor, immobilized by a karate hold. One man put his knee in my chest and the other, reaching back from the front seat, hit me in my kidneys and then punched me in the head to make me open my mouth and spit out the paper. At one point I felt I would never leave that car.

"This is as far as you're going, Yoani, I've had enough of your antics," said one while pulling my hair. In the back seat a rare spectacle: My legs were sticking up, my face red from the pressure, my body aching, while on the other side Orlando, brought down by a professional at beating people up. In an act of desperation I managed to grab the testicles of one of them through his trousers. I dug my nails in, thinking he was going to crush my chest. "Kill me now," I screamed, with my last breath, and the one in front warned the younger one, "Let her breathe."

I was listening to Orlando panting as the blows continued to rain down on us. I planned to open the door and throw myself out but there was no handle on the inside. We were at their mercy. Hearing Orlando's voice encouraged me. Later he told me it was the same for him hearing my choking words... it let him know, "Yoani is still alive." Finally they left us lying in a street in Timba, aching. A woman approached, "What happened?"... "A kidnapping," I managed to say. We cried in each others arms in the middle of the sidewalk, I thinking about Teo, for God's sake how am I going to explain all these bruises. How am I going to tell him that we live in a country where this can happen. How will I look at him and tell him that his mother has been beaten up on a public street for writing a blog, for putting her opinions in kilobytes. How can I describe the despotic faces of those who forced us into that car, their visible enjoyment as they beat us, their lifting my skirt as they dragged me half-naked to the car.

I managed to see, however, the degree of fright in our assailants, a fear of the new, of what they cannot destroy because they don't understand it, the blustering terror of those who know their days are numbered.

A brief medical report

I am recovering from the injuries inflicted during the abduction of last Friday. The bruises are lessening. What bothers me most now is a sharp pain in the lumbar region and I am using a crutch. Last night I went to the clinic where I was treated me for pain and inflammation. It's nothing that my youth and good health cannot overcome. Fortunately, the blow with which they forced my head to the floor of the car did not affect my eye, only my cheekbone and brow. I hope to recover in a few days.

A thank-you to friends and family who have looked after me. The effects are fading, even the psychological ones, which are the hardest. Orlando and Claudia are still in shock, but they are incredibly strong and also will overcome it. We have already begun to smile, the best medicine against abuse. The principal therapy for me remains this blog and the thousands of topics still waiting to be written about.

Shadow beings

After what happened last Friday, I have decided to post a series of pictures of the people who watch and harass me.

My relationship with the movies has always been from the seats, hearing the whirr of an old projector. Then I started to live in my own movie, a type of thriller with pursuers and the pursued, where it is up to me to escape and hide. The reason for this sudden change from spectator to protagonist has been this blog, located in this wide space—so little touched by celluloid—that is the Internet. Two years ago I woke up with the desire to write the true script of my days, not the rosy comedy shown in the official newspapers. I went, then, from watching movies to inhabiting one.

I have my doubts whether someday I'll see the curtain come down and be able to leave the movie theater alive. The decades-long film we've been living in Cuba doesn't seem to be close to the credit roll and a blank screen. However, spectators are no longer interested in the interminable filmstrip shown by the authorized projectionist. Rather, they seem captivated by the vision of those who create a blog, a blank page where they record questions, frustrations, and joys of actual citizens.

Believing myself a Kubrick or a Tarantino, I have begun to post images of these creatures who watch and harass us. Beings from the shadows who, like vampires, feed on our human happiness and fill us with terror through punches, threats, and blackmail. Individuals, trained in coercion, who did not anticipate their conversion from hunters to hunted, their faces trapped on cameras, mobile phones, or in the curious eyes of a citizen. Accustomed to gathering evidence for dossiers, records compiled on each of us, kept in some drawer in some office, now they are surprised that we make an inventory of their gestures and their eyes, and a meticulous record of their abuses.

The latest object of worship

Several years ago the State proclaimed the "Energy Revolution." The official media announced an immediate distribution of pressure cookers which, despite requiring electricity, would reduce the national consumption of petroleum. State industry began to manufacture rubber gaskets for the lids, which had formerly been made by private industry and sold at extortionate prices.

With the precision of a military operation, dozens of trucks took to the streets to distribute the new equipment. "Buy now, pay later" was the slogan. Skeptics did ask, however, how we were going to get the food to put in this new technology. But it was a time of widespread hope which, like love, seemed to come from the kitchen.

It unfolded like previous projects: At first the distribution went well, but the pots didn't quite make it into all households, nor were they well received everywhere. In some areas where pots were sold, natural gas service was immediately terminated and there were power outages at the most inconvenient times. And something else, unforeseen by the enthusiasts, happened. There were many people who could not afford these appliances. Lists of defaulters are still posted in local markets.

These pots, the latest object of worship from a paternalistic government, are no longer sold. Neither are the rubber gaskets which, once again, are available only on the black market for whatever price dealers care to demand.

Health update, November 15, 2009: I have regained my capacity to walk on two legs, abandoned the crutch, and

returned to my daily life. My thanks go to all of you who offered your hands in solidarity, the balm of support and the
effective medicine of your friendship.

Made in the USA

A few days ago the foreign press revealed that Spanish
Foreign Minister Miguel Angel Moratinos traveled to Havana with a message from the American administration. It
suggested that our leaders should improve civil liberties
in order to move in the direction of ending the dispute
between our countries. This message was not mentioned
in the official Cuban media. During Moratinos' visit, the
media heightened critiques of economic sanctions imposed
by the United States. These trade restrictions, so clumsy
and anachronistic in my judgment, are used to justify the
setbacks in productivity and to repress those who think differently. I am struck, however, by the fact that on market
shelves labels and packages reveal what the anti-imperialist
rhetoric hides: Much of what we eat says, "Made in
USA."

Never before have we had so much riding on the ups
and downs of Washington and Wall Street. The vaunted
sovereignty of this Island and the supposed example of
independence we show to the rest of the world hides how
dependent we really are on that nation where thousands of
our compatriots live. While the political slogans against the
Yankees grow stronger, people are more and more interested in the exchange between the two shores. The Florida
Straits seem to separate us, but in fact there is an invisible

bridge of affection, material aid, and information that links this island to the mainland.

The poor cobbler, born a few years before the United States broke relations with our country, fixes the shoes with glue sent to him by a brother in Miami. The flash memory the young man wears around his neck is from a "Yuma," an American, who docked his yacht at the Hemingway marina; the corner hairdresser sends to New Jersey for her dyes and creams. Without this flow of products and remittances, many people around me would be begging and neglected. Even the whiskey that the highest Party leaders drink exhibits the unmistakable seal of the forbidden.

Soft diet

Adolfo Fernández Sainz lives among stories like the one he sent us below. Adolfo turned sixty-one yesterday, with the last six of those years spent locked in a Canaleta prison cell, ever since the Black Spring of 2003.

That afternoon the last of his canine teeth would be extracted. He had spent days on it, helped by another inmate skilled in extracting teeth, even molars. The collection of what was pulled was put under the pillow, and it would stay there until the time came to throw the teeth, with their yellow enamel, through the tiny window of the cell.

If all went as expected, the coming week he would be showing his smooth-gummed mouth to the doctor. He would say they had fallen out, as had happened to a character in the film *Papillon*, which he'd seen when he was a boy. In that film, a prisoner had suffered from scurvy, but he, no.

He had renounced his teeth to get access to the soft diet given prisoners who cannot chew. The preparation of plantain and sweet potato was more flavorful than the rancid food served to the others. So it was a question of survival to do without these useless things surrounding his tongue.

Cojo (The Cripple) had prepared the instruments as if he had a diploma in dentistry. Before going to Cojo's bunk, he studied his canine for the last time in the polished tin that served as a mirror. There was nothing to be sorry about; it was full of cavities, twisted to the right and stained with nicotine. This tiny obstacle was not going to stand between food and his needy body. He gave it a few knocks to loosen it and walked over to where several prisoners were also waiting for an extraction. On the mattress, a piece of a spoon and a small metal bar would take the place of a hammer and chisel to weaken the tooth; an improvised pair of pliers, made from two pieces of wire, would remove the root. Payment for the makeshift surgery would be cigarettes, about twenty he had saved after many days of not smoking.

Later he would go to sleep with the throbbing around the hole that had once sheltered his eyetooth, happy to be able to join the brotherhood of the toothless. Others in their beds would also be controlling pain, dreaming all night of an aluminum tray brimming over with soft puree.

Anemic arguments

On December 10 a mob assaulted women who had only gladioli in their hands. Fists raised—urged on by plainclothes police—they surrounded these mothers, wives and daughters of those imprisoned since the Black Spring of 2003. Several of the attackers learned the script on the run, and they mixed current political slogans with those popular almost three decades ago. It was a shock troop with license to insult and beat, granted by precisely those whose job it is to maintain order and protect all citizens. On Friday's newscast the announcer said that those who berated the Women in White represented an "enraged people," but on the screen there was no hint of spontaneity or real conviction. It just looked like fanatics who were afraid, very afraid.

I'm ashamed to say it, but in my country the demons of intolerance were having a party on Human Rights Day. Those who long ago lost the ability to convince and win us over with a new and just idea, had incited them. They don't even have an ideology any more, they just keep their hands on the reins of fear and call for "exemplary" acts of repudiation to stem growing discontent. On the faces of those summoned to do the social lynching, one could see doubt alternating with rage, exaltation with a fear of being observed and judged. As painful as it may be, it's easy to foresee that perhaps one day a multitude just as blind and unthinking might direct their anger against those who, today, pit some Cubans against others.

Lacking economic openness, more food on the plate, structural changes, or long-awaited relaxations, Raúl Castro's government seems to have chosen punishment as the formula for self-preservation. There are no other tangible results of his management. Rather, there are the sounds of the rusty instruments of control and the old techniques of punishment. They haven't even put forth promises of projects or announced plans with imprecise dates. Rather, they reach for their belt, not to tighten it in a gesture of austerity and savings, but to use it as authoritarian parents do, on the hides of their children.

2010

The last moon of 2009

At midnight I threw the traditional bucket of water from
my balcony, in a ritual act of cleansing to expel everything
that keeps our nation from advancing. This morning, the
first sun of 2010 dried the puddles around all the buildings.
The streams of water sounded like a cataract as they left every house. "Let the bad go, let it go," we thought, in unison,
millions of Cubans.

Reggaeton

More than five years ago, a sensual and extroverted rhythm
flooded the country's nightclubs and discos, accompanied
by an unabashed physicality openly expressing a desire for
fun, sex, and the good life. Salsa bands adapted their music
and wrote new lyrics to the reggaeton beat. The songs are
clearly erotic, and yet they describe an area of Cuban reality without triumphalism or whitewash. In the east a hard-
edged, more direct style, known as "perreo," has spun off.

It's rare to find a taxi or bicycle-taxi anywhere on the
island that doesn't feature, at full volume, catchy tunes
that show no signs of dying out. One of the most interesting things about reggaeton is how little it resembles the
socially-conscious music of the sixties and seventies. If the

songwriters of that era alluded constantly to their dedication, willingness, and desire to contribute to the social process, today's music shows an attraction to the material, a focus on satisfying immediate desires. The music comes from a process of change much more complex than just a couple of chords or some new dance steps.

Onstage a group of boys repeats almost to hysteria, "¡Mami, goza!" while the crowd sways and sweats under colored lights. Many criticize these new rhythms, tied as they are to foreign currents and consumerism, but the fans of reggaeton care little. For them, a resounding chorus that calls for enjoyment is—like it or not—the new anthem of these times.

Our daily problem

I go out dressed in several sweaters with an ancient scarf around my neck. The errand is short, but the temperature is so low that every step I take feels like a great sacrifice. People beside me in the street are equally "disguised." I even see someone with a blanket wrapped around his shoulders. It's a short trip to the bakery and I don't see anyone wearing a nice coat. But popular inventiveness does not end when the mercury falls. The Soviet-era raincoats, with their enormous buttons and now-faded colors, have been dusted off. Others, who have nothing to wrap up in, simply stay home.

I head toward the non-rationed bakery, where a loaf of bread costs a whole day's wages. Many people, in their strange and improvised costumes, are headed in the same direction. Everyone is going for of the same staple food that has kept us in suspense for several weeks now. A few feet from the shop, someone up ahead cries out, "It's all gone!" It's like she's thrown a bucket of cold water on us all. I turn around and go home. Tomorrow will be another day without breakfast.

The arrival of this cold has coincided with the disappearance not only of bread, but also of milk. As if winter breaks the ovens and freezes the cows' udders. On TV they announce that milk production has exceeded targets, yet there is none for our morning coffee or insipid tea. These are times to jerk yourself awake, look away from the table, tell the kids not to ask questions, and put aside all work, the blog, friends, life, to devote yourself entirely to the pursuit of a piece of bread and a glass of milk. Time to drag yourself through the dust of shortages and lines. Because to break this contemptible cycle, to be able to fly, we need—more than wings—food.

Naming the children

"What do you think we should name him?" asks my friend, six months pregnant and expecting a baby boy. My first impulse is to respond with the usual, "José," but her scowl makes me try to think of something less traditional. I run through the full catalog, including Mateo, Lázaro, and Fabián, but none pleases the expectant mother. If it were twenty years ago, the baby would have to carry around a "Y" name. However, the exotic habit of using the penultimate letter of the alphabet seems to have been conquered.

For some decades, Cubans named their children with

a freedom they did not experience in other spheres in life. The grayness that the ration market and state control spread over our existence vanished when we inscribed our newborns' names in the civil register. Parents played with language and created real tongue-twisters, such as the famous baseball player: "Vicyohandri." A few even came up with the unusual composition "Yesdasí," a mix of the English, Russian, and Spanish words for "yes."

Fortunately, in recent years calmer winds blow when it comes time to name a child. An entire generation now prefers to go back to the old ways. So, after several days, my friend calls to tell me her decision: Juan Carlos. On the other end of the line, I breathe a sigh of relief. Sanity has returned.

El Corralito

Every night, in a luxury hotel cabaret, a European businessman goes from table to table with an unusual request. He asks guests to let him pay their bills with the colored vouchers in his pocket. They then give him the amount in convertible pesos, which he can turn into dollars or euros and take out of the country. This man is a victim of the financial "Corralito" which prevents many foreign investors from taking their earnings out of the country.[28] So that they don't utterly despair, Cuban authorities allow them to consume from one end of the Island to the other, paying with pieces of paper lacking any real worth.

This drama of frozen funds affects many businessmen who, after the Foreign Investment Law of 1995, were ready to invest in our economy. They enjoyed the privilege of running a company, completely forbidden to those born here. They became a new business class in a country where the Revolutionary Offensive of 1968 confiscated even the shoeshine boys' chairs. Huge profits made them attractive targets for hustlers, landlords, and members of State Security. Many frequented the most expensive restaurants and enjoyed appetizing dishes, young women at their sides. Others, the minority, supplemented their employees' very low wages—paid in Cuban pesos by the State, which contracted out their labor—with generous gifts.

These business represented a "corporate scouting party," prepared to lose a little capital to establish themselves in a country that would eventually be shared out like slices of pie. But to those on the Island who signed the contracts and drank their champagne, they were no more than a necessary and temporary evil, something that would be eradicated as soon as the Special Period ended. After all the promises and guarantees, the coffers are now empty, and all they hear is, "We cannot pay you."

Suddenly, these businessmen are feeling the impotence—the scream half-stuck in the throat—with which Cubans are burdened every day. Still, unlike us they are protected against the depredation of the State; with their foreign passports they can board a plane and forget everything.

Repairs

Domestic life imposes unpleasant obligations. The faucet leaks, the lamp refuses to light, the lock on the door sticks, and one evil day (horrors!) the refrigerator breaks down. Terrified, we discover that the freezer is dripping and the appliance's typical humming sound is no more. My neighbor, José Antonio, lived through a tragedy of this magnitude last week.

Early in the morning he called the nearest Domestic Repair Unit, but either they didn't answer or he got a busy signal. So he decided to go there. The receptionist was meticulously polishing her fingernails. Distressed, he told her the story of his appliance and described its symptoms. He was about to venture a diagnosis but she interrupted him, saying that surely it was the timer and that they didn't have the spare part. Not only that, the workshop had a waiting list months long. Like a savvy man with some real-life experience, José formulated the correct question in a suitable tone: "And is there no other way to resolve this?" The woman paused in her manicure and shouted to a mechanic.

After agreeing on a price, everyone was satisfied. By midday the refrigerator was working again and the repairman went home with the equivalent of nearly two month's wages. That night, my neighbor, who is a barman at a five-star hotel, took several bottles of rum purchased on the black market with him to work. With these, he made the first of the tourists' mojitos and tasty piña coladas. They had no idea they were helping fill the enormous hole in José Antonio's budget left by the refrigerator repair.

Much more frightened than I am

This Friday, January 29, was complicated from the start. In

the morning, Claudio, a photography professor at the Blogger Academy, went missing. We later learned he'd been arrested by an agent who barely deigned to show him a card with the initials DES (Department of State Security).

Later, we had a little celebration at our house after classes for the first anniversary of *Voces Cubanas*—which in its brief life has grown to twenty-six sites. In the middle of the hugs and smiles, someone told me to be careful. I told him, "In today's system, there is no way to protect oneself from attacks from the State," trying to frighten away my own fear.

Around six in the evening we headed out to celebrate my sister's thirty-six birthday. My father heard her first cry early on the day set aside to honor railroad workers. Even Teo, with his adolescent reluctance to participate in "old people's" activities, agreed to come with us. We were expecting the usual party, with photos, candles to blow out, and "Happy birthday to you, Yunia, may you enjoy many more." But lurking eyes had another plan for us. On Boyeros Avenue, a few yards from the Ministry of the Interior and Raúl Castro's office, three cars stopped our miserable Russian Lada taxi.

"Don't even think about going to Twenty-third Street, Yoani, because the Union of Young Communists is having an event," shouted the men who got out of the Chinese-made Geely, which reminded me of a sharp pain in my lumbar zone. I had already lived through something similar last November. Today I will not allow them to put me head-first into another car, with my son.

A huge man got out of the vehicle and started to repeat

his threats, "What is your name?" Reinaldo kept asking. The man never bothered to respond. From Teo's lanky body rose the ironic phrase, "He doesn't say his name because he is a coward." Worse still, Teo, worse still, he doesn't say his name because he is not recognized as an individual, but simply as a voice for others, much higher up. A professional camera filmed our every move, waiting for an aggressive pose, a vulgar phrase, an excess of anger. This injection of terror was brief. We arrived at the birthday bitter.

How can we emerge unscathed from all this? How can a citizen protect himself from a State that has the police, the courts, the Rapid Response Brigades, the mass media, the capacity to defame and lie, the power to socially lynch him and turn him into someone defeated and apologetic? What were they thinking would happen today on Twenty-third Street that would make them arrest several bloggers?

I feel a terror that almost doesn't let me type. But I want to tell those who threatened me and my family today, when one reaches a certain level of panic, higher doses don't make any difference. I will not stop writing, or Twittering; I have no plans to close my blog, nor abandon the practice of thinking independently, and—above all—I will not stop believing that they are much more frightened than I am.

Protect your own, steal from others

At night he watches over the furrows of malanga and the flock of lambs with a short, homemade shotgun. The gun is the improvised work of a gunsmith who welded a small-diameter piece of pipe to a rustic chamber. The sound of this ingenious device is enough to scare off anyone who tries to steal the harvest. When the sow gives birth, he calls his brother, and with this contraption, created by necessity, they keep watch until sunrise.

Many farmers use illegal weapons that have been purchased or produced in an alternative way. Without them, the fruits of months of labor could end up in the hands of the "predators" of grain, shadows that move in darkness. Poverty has increased stealing in the countryside and forced villagers to safeguard resources. Hence the proliferation of attack dogs and shotguns, particularly on farms where there are cows. A pound of beef selling for two convertible pesos on the black market rewards the thefts and illegal slaughter, despite the threat of lengthy prison sentences.

For these guardians, an official announcement came as a surprise: "... in exceptional circumstances and only once [...] people native to and residing legally on the island, and who have in their control unlicensed firearms, will be able to obtain the required registration."

But people believe that whoever publicly admits to possessing a firearm will find it confiscated. Given this fear, few confess, preferring the risk of not having papers to the insecurity of being left without protection. To our alarm, these rustic tools also serve those who have neither farms nor animals to protect, who lie in wait on the other side of the fence, inclined to take what belongs to others.

The instant creation of emerging teachers

It was a sober meeting, attended by representatives of the municipal Ministry of Education. A murmur passed among parents seated in children's plastic chairs. The announcement of who would continue to senior secondary school was approaching, and at this meeting they would tell us the number of pre-university or technical-school slots assigned to our school. We weren't expecting the elimination of "comprehensive general teachers"; we believed that they would continue to exist at least until our great-grandchildren reached puberty.

Training adolescents to teach classes ranging from grammar to mathematics ends in complete failure. Not because of their youth, which is always welcome in any profession, but because of the haste of their training and their almost universal lack of interest.

The emerging teachers program was developed in response to the mass exodus of educators to other jobs with more attractive earnings. But with this program, the already ailing quality of Cuban education fell through the floor. Children came home saying that Cuba had "a civil war" in 1895, not a war of independence, and that geometric figures had something called "voldes" which we parents understood to mean "edges." I remember one instant educator who confessed to his students on the first day of class that they should "Study hard so you don't end up like me, someone who ended up being a teacher because I didn't take good notes."

Then came the tele-classes, filling a very high percentage of school hours with a cold TV screen that cannot interact with students. The idea was to make up for the instant teachers' lack of training. Teacher salaries increased symbolically, but they never exceeded the equivalent of thirty dollars a month. Thus, being a teacher became even more of a sacrifice than being a priest.

There were young people who signed a pledge to become teachers but regretted it after one week of work, people at the front of the classroom who had not yet mastered spelling or the history of their own country. The educational deformations wrought by this plan are written in the hidden book of failures of revolutionary plans and ridiculous production goals. The difference is that, we are not talking about tons of sugar or bushels of beans, but the education of our children.

I breathe a sigh of relief that this long experiment in education has ended. But I don't foresee a day when teachers will leave the steering wheels of their taxis, come out from behind the bars, or exchange the tedium of working at home to return to the classroom. I would feel better, though, if in place of a television screen an actual teacher, with a mastery of content, taught Teo's classes. I think for that we will have to wait for the great-grandchildren.

GPS

Speaking of the emigration talks between Cuba and the United States taking place today in Havana, Carlitos finally made it to Atlanta, after trying five times to cross the Florida Straits. On two occasions he was intercepted by the US Coast Guard and returned to the Island, and for months he saved the yellow form they gave him to request—legally—a visa from the US Interest Section. He was also captured by the Cubans, on August 13 three years ago, when his boat's propeller broke. That trip ended in a jail in the village of Cojimar. He was fined and plainclothes officers began to visit him, demanding that he find a job. However, he preferred a faster way to leave behind police harassment and the room he shared with his grandmother.

This young man of thirty-two, after showing his negligible talents as a sailor, managed to get to Ecuador, one of a few countries that don't require visas. This Latin American nation was his trampoline to enter the United States, where he is now starting a new life.

He left his GPS with some friends who had helped him, along with that form he had never filled out asking for a humanitarian visa. He did not leave with a fixed idea in mind; rather he feared becoming a frustrated forty-year-old. Not even on his most optimistic days could he foresee that in Cuba he would have his own roof, or a salary that would allow him to avoid having to steal from the State to survive.

Like so many others, Carlitos harbored no hope that promises made to him as a child would ever be kept. He did not want to grow old sitting on the sidewalk in front of his house, taking the edge off his failure with alcohol or pills. He planned every kind of escape, but finally his uncle paid for a ticket to Quito with the idea that he would get the rest of the family out. He still has nightmares about boats that take him back to Cuba in handcuffs, smelling of salt and oil. He wakes up and looks around to confirm that he is still in the little apartment he rented with a girlfriend. "Once

a rafter, always a rafter," he muses, turning his pillow over
and trying to dream on solid ground.

Chance

You could have been a prostitute selling your favors, or an
interrogator for State Security. The needs were so many
that to exchange your body for a bottle of shampoo or
some soap was always a possibility. Except that your body
was too frail to trade and your skin too pale for foreigners
who came looking for the cinnamon they'd seen in tourist
ads. Also, you lacked a "certain something" to carry off the
tight-fitting garments used to exchange sex for money, or
to strut around outside some hotel to get your family out
of a tight spot.

At the end of ninth grade you almost donned a uniform to go to Camilo Cienfuegos military school, to escape
a house with too many prohibitions and too much misery.
You thought you were ready to become a pursed-lipped soldier, with all those little privileges enjoyed by the Army and
the Interior Ministry. A friend's advice made you abandon
shouts of "Ah-ten-SHUN!" and the constant rattle of a machine gun. But if you had not heard her question, "What
will you do with yourself, wedged between orders and
trenches?" perhaps you would now be intimidating a political prisoner in a closed room at Villa Marista.

You could have been a rafter, a suicide, a government
minister's lover, a censor, a political prisoner, a cop, or a victim. It was not possible to emerge unscathed from the crisis
of the nineties—the collapse of values, the marginal scene

where you came of age. Some part of you was left in red ly-
cra standing on the corner, or in the epaulettes of a lieutenant. You could have been any of these people, but by chance,
by events, and by your own weariness, you were saved.

Wanting to scream

February 27, 2010 : Life never returns to normal. It does not
go back to a time before the tragedy, a time we now evoke
as a period of calm. I open my datebook, try to resume my
life, the blog, the Twitter messages… but nothing comes
out. These last days have been too intense. The face of
Reina Tamayo, in the shadows in front of the morgue where
she prepared and dressed her son for his longest journey, is
the only thing in my mind. Then the images of Wednesday
pile on: arrests, beatings, violence, a jail cell with the stink
of urine that adjoined another from which Eugenio Leal
and Ricardo Santiago demanded their rights. The rest of
the time I continue on like an automaton, looking without
seeing, furiously typing.

And so, there is no one here who can write a coherent
and restrained line. I so want to scream, but February 24
left me hoarse.

Testimony from Orlando Zapata Tamayo's mother

February 23, 2010: This afternoon, hours after the death of
Orlando Zapata Tamayo, Reinaldo and I were able to approach the Department of Legal Medicine in Boyeros Street,
where autopsies are performed.

A detail from State Security was watching the place, but we managed to approach Reina, Orlando's mother, and ask her the questions whose answers are posted below. Pain, indignation in our case... sadness and fortitude in hers.

YOANI SÁNCHEZ: We are here to express our condolences. We would like to know at what time did he pass away, what do you know about his last minutes, what are your feelings right now, and what is going to happen after he is released by the coroner?

REINA LUISA TAMAYO DANGER: I am Reina Luisa Tamayo Danger, the mother of prisoner of conscience Orlando Zapata Tamayo, who was interned in the hospital of the Habana del Este Prison. Last night he was moved to the Hermanos Ameijeiras Hospital, where he passed away at 3:00 p.m.

I can tell you I feel a horrible pain, but I am hanging on, enduring through this pain. I was able to be at his side until he passed away and now I hope to have the courage to dress my son, Orlando Zapata Tamayo.

We will leave for Banes, Holguin Province, Embarcadero Road, house number six, where we will hold the wake before our family altar, at my home, for as long as required.

I want to tell the world about my pain. I think my son's death was a premeditated murder. My son was tortured throughout his incarceration. His plight has brought me great pain and has been excruciating for the entire family. Even as he was transferred to this prison, he was first held in Camaguey without drinking water for eighteen days.

My son died after an eighty-six-day hunger strike. He is another Pedro Boitel for Cuba. [Pedro Luis Boitel died in 1972 during a hunger strike while serving a ten-year prison sentence in Cuba.]

In the midst of deep pain, I call on the world to demand the freedom of the other prisoners and brothers unfairly sentenced so that what happened to my boy, my second child, who leaves behind no physical legacy, no child or wife, does not happen again. Thank you!

Reporting the news... living the news

To write about what hurts us, to report on what we have encountered, touched, and suffered, transcends journalism and becomes living testimony. The distance between articles about a man on a hunger strike and the act of feeling his ribs protruding from his sides, is an abyss. Thus, no interview can reproduce the tear-filled eyes of Clara, Guillermo "Coco" Fariñas' wife, while she tells me that Guillermo, a journalist himself, grows thinner every day. No reporting can describe the panic caused by the camera posted a hundred yards from their home that observes and films everyone who approaches 615A Calle Alemán.

Taking notes and recording video fail to convey the odor of the emergency room to which Fariñas was moved yesterday. My guilt for coming too late to beg him to eat again, to persuade him to stop this irreversible damage to his health, is unbearable. On the drive there, I wove together some phrases to convince him not to carry on to the end. But before I arrived a text message told me he was already hospitalized. I would have said to him, "You have already accomplished it, you have helped to remove their mask," but instead I offer words of consolation to his family, who sit in his absence in their room in the humble neighborhood of La Chirusa.

Why have they brought us to this point? How can they close down all paths to dialog, debate, healthy dissent, and necessary criticism? With this kind of protest, a protest of empty stomachs, we have to question whether they have left citizens any other way to show their lack of consent. Fariñas knew they would never give him one minute on the radio. His voice could not rise up, without penalty, in a public place. Refusing to eat was the only way he found to show the desperation and despair of living under a system that gags and masks his most important accomplishments.

Coco cannot die. Because in the long funeral procession that has taken Orlando Zapata Tamayo, our voice, and the rights of citizens killed long ago... there is no room for one more death.

Tropical mafia

A deluge of events is raining on Cuba. The first drops fell at the beginning of January, with the deaths from starvation and cold of several dozen patients in the Havana Psychiatric Hospital. The flood intensified with the death of Orlando Zapata Tamayo, pushed to his end by the negligence of jailers and the stubbornness of our leaders. Then came the hunger strike of the journalist Guillermo Fariñas, and with it our lives fell into the center of a political tornado whose hurricane winds are increasing every day.

Along with these tempests, a series of corruption scandals have come as a check on the powerful. According to rumors, allegations have come to light about ministers who had suitcases full of dollars hidden in water tanks, commercial flights whose dividends went into the hands of a few, and juice factories whose enormous earnings were quickly rushed out of the country. Among those implicated appear to be men who came down from the Sierra Maestra in 1959, who now enrich themselves by awarding licenses to foreign companies who repay them with succulent commissions. The State has been looted by the State itself. The diversion of resources is at a level at which the filching of milk from a warehouse looks like child's play. The powerful on the Island take to the road with stuffed suitcases, as if they sense that today's downpour will eventually bring the roof down on their own heads. We are a country in the midst of a liquidation sale, while many wearing the olive-green uniform take the opportunity to make off with what little we have left.

A complicit press, meanwhile, speaks of past glories and important anniversaries, and declares that the Revolution has never been stronger. Behind the curtain, a series of purges are carried out. Auditors dig into the guts of our finances and confirm that nothing can be done before the advancing corruption. The "historic" generation has not only showed us how to live a complete masquerade; it has also shown that the nation's coffers are their personal wallet. Wastewaters of ethical and moral misery, that they themselves created and from which they prospered, appear about to drown us all.

DHL or how to help the censor

A couple of years ago I went to the DHL office in Miramar to send some family videos to friends in Spain. The clerk looked at me as if I were asking to send a molecule of oxygen to another galaxy. Without even touching the mini-cassette, she told me that the Havana branch only accepted VHS. I thought it was a question of size, but the explanation she gave was even more surprising: "It's just that our machines to view the content only read the large cassettes." When I tried to insist, the woman suspected that I wanted to send "enemy propaganda" abroad rather than the smiling face of my son.

Frustrated, I returned home—where I've never received a piece of regular mail—and some time passed before I again turned to this German company. Because I was not allowed to travel to Chile for publication of my book there, the publisher sent me ten copies a few days ago in an "express" package. Neither my numerous phone calls to the DHL office nor my physically going there, over and over, resulted in their delivering to me what is mine. This morning they told me, "Your package has been confiscated." They should have been more honest and confessed, "Your package has been stolen." Despite the fact that the book is the same collection of words I've published on the Web for the last three years, Customs has treated it like a how-to manual for Molotov cocktails.

Although headlines around the world announce the end of Google's collusion with Chinese censorship, foreign companies in Cuba continue to obey the government's imposed ideological filters. Despite its air of efficiency, its tradition of speed, and its motto of "We keep an eye on your package," DHL applies a political filter to its customers. They would be thrown out of the country if they didn't—with the consequent economic loss. So they ignore the sanctity of the mail and look away when someone demands what belongs to her. Their brown-and-yellow corporate colors never seemed so strident to me. But today I feel that, instead of promising speed and efficiency, they should admit: "Your mail isn't safe, even with us!"

Fame and applause

For over a decade, at the corner of Infanta and Manglar, stood the unfinished mass of a twenty-story building. Its construction ran aground on the Special Period and the end of construction "microbrigades." The people who laid the foundation, believing they would get an apartment in the high-rise, raged with impotence when construction stopped. They gave years of their lives to build those walls, and suddenly the wished-for home escaped with the speed of the Soviet technicians who boarded planes to their homeland.

With its incomplete twenty floors still surrounded by construction materials, the building was one of the new ruins that adorn our city. Due to the enormous housing shortages, many planned to occupy it illegally and avoid the disaster-relief shelters from some cyclone-gone-by. But the site was well guarded. Some ministry was cooking up a plan to restart the work and award the apartments. Neighbors saw them return with cranes, trucks, and cement, and a few construction workers who would not be allowed to live there after it opened. Rather than to the original micro-brigade members, ownership would be awarded based on political, artistic, or journalistic merit. We all understood the plan: The building at Infanta and Manglar would be awarded to the Party faithful.

So, in the midst of the campaign to bring Elián González back to Cuba, we saw some particularly enthusiastic voices immediately compensated with a key to a new home. Popular cunning baptized the finished building, "Fame and Applause," after the TV show. It began to fill with singers, film directors, cartoonists, ministers, reporters, and actors. Participating in the "Battle of Ideas" now had a concrete result: a window with a view of the impoverished district of San Martín. For many, finally getting their own home made them toe the official line all the more willingly. The illuminated parking lot was filling fast with new cars, completing the residents' already-substantial package of perks.

The eyes that peek out of the humble dwellings next door are surprised that the old ruin is now a huge gleaming mass, freshly painted, with anti-glare glass, and famous faces looking out of each window.

From milk to the parapets

With the mass exodus of foreign investors, the store shelves

show the real state of our finances. My mother called early
to tell me there is toilet paper at a distant market; she said
to hurry because word was already out and it would soon
be gone. I look everywhere for some juice to put in Teo's
cup in the morning, but the shortage of supplies is remark-
able and Río Zaza brand Tetra Paks have disappeared from
the shops because the joint venture that produced them
is mired in a corruption scandal. The black market, once
fed by diverting resources from the factories and stealing
goods being transported to markets, has collapsed.

Even the most patient foreign entrepreneurs, such as
the outstanding Spanish firm Vima, have packed their bags
and gone home. The consortium of perfume maker Suchel
and Camacho has come to an end, leaving my friends—now
without hair dyes—showing their gray. The time when the
country bought first and paid later is over and we now carry
so much debt that it is difficult to attract capital or to buy
on credit. The effects of the crisis are felt strongly in everyday life, with the price of soap 30 percent more than it
was a year ago. Housewives scratch their heads when faced
with the skillet, while shouting that wages go like water.
Not even those blessed with a remittance from abroad or
traders in the informal market have it easy.

Few remember Raúl Castro's "glass of milk for every
Cuban" speech, and his speech last Sunday brought us
images of trenches, parapets, and an island sinking into
the sea. Chasing elusive food, we have little time to think
about what goes on at the Palace of Conventions, but Raúl's
Numantian threat hangs over us: Cuba would rather die
than change. His speech evokes a foxhole surrounded by

sandbags, a rifle to shoot we don't know whom, and a final bullet reserved for ourselves. Meanwhile, the General stands firmly at his post, checking from a distance that all obey the final order of self-destruction.

The stigma of prosperity

For Cubans of my generation, longing for success was a terrible ideological deviation—not only longing to stand out personally, but professionally and economically. We were raised to be humble, and if we received any kind of recognition, we were taught to emphasize that we could not have achieved it without the help of our comrades. It was the same with the simple possession of an object, the enjoyment of a comfort, or the "unhealthy" ambition to prosper.

Competitiveness was punished with accusations very difficult to expunge from our dossiers, accusations such as "self-sufficient" or "immodest." Success must be—or be seen to be—shared, the fruit of everyone's labors under the wise direction of the Party. And so we learned that self-esteem must be hidden and enterprising enthusiasm reined in. The mediocre made a killing in this society while conformity clipped the wings of the most daring. We hid material possessions to show that we were all children of a self-sacrificing proletariat, and that we detested the bourgeoisie.

Some faked egalitarianism as they accumulated privileges and amassed fortunes—while repeating in their speeches the calls for austerity. We heard again and again that they came from poor families and their main aspiration was to serve the Fatherland. In time, their colleagues

discovered that hidden behind the ascetic image was someone who diverted State resources or compulsively accumulated possessions. Even today, the mask of frugality covers
their faces while their bulging abdomens tell a completely
different story.

Inflated payrolls

"Ending the inflated payrolls" is the latest of the never-end-
ing list of remedies to help our failing economy. But those
who will be left without jobs call it something else: Unemployment. Lengthy TV reports tell us that the problem is
too many employees in offices, factories, and even hospitals.
Each workday must contain enough work to avoid idleness,
they report, as if this notion was discovered just last week.

Some economists warn that unemployment figures
could soar to more than 25 percent. One in four workers
will be laid off from the bloated payrolls because the country has no liquidity to pay idle hands. Such a high number
would suggest an increase in social unrest, and hundreds
of thousands of people would take up illegal occupations,
while the trick of under-employment would be used to
skew employment statistics. For reasons of image, people
without jobs will not be called "unemployed" but something more subtle, such as "surplus" or "idled."

I would like to see what is going to happen in government departments swarming with bureaucrats, or in the
inflated department of State Security. Will they also be
downsizing? Seeing the growing number of plainclothes
police on the streets, I think they could start there.

Twitter: that wild beast

Last night a friend from Las Villas visited. To reach the capital, he must overcome transportation troubles and the surveillance that follows him. He told me that he was detained a few weeks ago and that they confiscated his mobile phone. Soon an officer appeared, annoyed, with the small Nokia in his hands. "Now you're in trouble," he kept saying. The reason: His phone's address book included an entry for Twitter, accompanied by a number in the UK.

"No one can save you from fifteen years," threatened the officer, assuring him that sending an SMS to a stranger with a strange name who lived so far away was a crime of enormous proportions. He did not know that our tweets get to the Internet via text-only messages sent from cellphones. Nor did he know that, rather than to British intelligence, our brief texts go to this blue bird that makes them fly through cyberspace. It is true, we broadcast blind and cannot read others' replies, but at least we are reporting on the Island in 140-character fragments.

Seeing conspiracies, agents, and plots everywhere, they haven't noticed that technology has turned every citizen into his or her own mass media. No longer is it only foreign correspondents who validate a story in the eyes of the world; increasingly it is our own Twitter reports. My friend put it this way: "Yoani, coming to Havana we had a big security detail behind us. I had a text message ready to send in case they stopped us." Perhaps it was the bright Nokia display that deterred them from forcing him into a patrol car. If they had, a brief click would have sent his shout across the Web instantly, alerting the world to what the international press would have taken hours to find out.

When I saw him off, he had his cellphone in hand like a dimly lit lantern. In the folder marked "drafts" was an already-prepared text to protect him from the shadows that waited for him below.

Dangerous liaisons

He restored all kinds of books, from Bibles to incunabula. He was very good at repairing the torn-out pages and covers and of treating pages with a chemical solution that highlighted ink. He had worked on nineteenth-century manuscripts, first editions of the works of José Martí, and even a couple of copies of the Constitution of 1940. He returned them all to their former elegance, and as he salvaged them he liked to read them, like a doctor wanting to peek into the soul of a patient whose viscera he already knows well.

He had never seen a book, though, like the one brought that afternoon in the late eighties. From its sheer size it seemed like a pharmacology text, but it contained no chemical formulas or medicines. Instead it was full of accusations. It was, in fact, a detailed inventory of all the reports that employees in a certain company had made against fellow workers. Without realizing her indiscretion, the director's secretary sent this enormous register of complaint to be repaired. Thus, this invaluable testimony of betrayal came into his hands.

Like the plot of *Dangerous Liaisons*, there was Alberto, the chief of personnel, accused of taking raw material for his house. A few pages later, Alberto himself told of the "counterrevolutionary" sentiments expressed by the dining-room cleaning assistant. Murmurs overlapped, weaving a real and frightful nest where everyone spied on everyone. Maricusa, the accountant—as witnessed by her office mate—was selling cigars from her desk. She, in turn, reported that the administrator left some hours before closing. A mechanic appeared several times for having an extramarital affair with a union woman, while several reports against the cook were signed in his own hand.

The restorer felt only enormous pain for these "characters" acting out this sinister, traitorous plot. He returned the book, after doing the worst job he had ever done. Even today, he can't stop thinking about the names, reports, and accusations of those pages, accumulating still, after all these years.

Squaring the circle

A friend pointed out strange colored dots on the bottom of soft drink and beer cans sold in cafes and restaurants. I looked closer and it was true—red on some, blue or green on others, all drawn with a marker. Even on the empty cans at the recycling center, the curious "seal" was there. The mark was not precise like from a machine, but rather was the unsteady stroke of a hand doing something forbidden.

Behind this colored dot is a lucrative network that uses State enterprises to sell private goods. Food-service employees buy canned drinks in hard-currency stores and then sell them where they work, marking up each one between

10 and 50 percent. During the work day they prioritize the sale of "their own" products, delaying the sale of those belonging to the State. At the end of the day, with the added centavos from each sale, they accrue dividends much greater than their purely symbolic salary paid in national currency.

The color of the dots indicates who owned what was sold. The local administrator might be red, the waitress blue, and the cook probably opted for orange. Everyone gets a share. If not, what would be the point of getting up early, riding a packed bus, and working eight hours for the equivalent of $20 US at the end of the month?

Regarding the beer market, clandestine factories produce Bucanero and Cristal-like beer, packaged exactly like the originals. Even long-time drinkers can hardly tell the difference. These knock-off industries are in what look like family homes. The products displace those made by the State—disloyal competitors to the great *Patrón*—stealing market share.

A labyrinthine network of counterfeiting and resale underlies this dysfunctional centralization and diverts profits into thousands of private pockets.

The route of the moisture

On the corner is a hydrant that is the only water supply for hundreds of families in the area. Even the water-carriers come to it with their fifty-five-gallon tanks on old rickety carts that clatter as they roll by. People wait for the thin stream to fill containers and then return home, with the children helping to push the wagon. Inhabitants of this

Central Havana neighborhood make this run every two days, when they tire of waiting for the pipes in their homes to bring something other than noise and cockroaches. They live in dilapidated tenements in the old mansions with ornamented walls and mold on the ceilings. The condition of the housing doesn't matter, nor whether it's the rainy season or a drought; the problem lies under the ground, in the water mains as old and worn out as their grandparents.

Residents who rent rooms to foreigners install motors known as "water thieves." At night, they pump the water that should supply the nearby houses into their own water tanks; it's the only way to guarantee that tourist guests can take a shower. If the water main breaks, they pay someone to lug several buckets from the nearest street, or buy from a water truck for the equivalent of a month's salary. For many in Havana, access to drinking water has been a question of purchasing power. Those who have more can open the tap and let it run while they wash their hands; those who have less rinse their mouths with the contents of a jar.

My last bit of faith

Over two months ago I filed a complaint of illegal detention, police violence, and arbitrary imprisonment. After the death of Orlando Zapata Tamayo, illegal arrests prevented more than one hundred people from participating in activities surrounding his funeral. I was among the many who ended up in jail that February 24, arrested on my way to sign the condolence book. The level of violence used, and the violation of arrest procedures, led me to file a claim, though with little hope that it would ever be heard in court. I have waited all this time, holding back revealing evidence about the violation of our rights, for a response from the Military Prosecutor and the Attorney General.

Fortunately, my cell phone recorded audio of what happened that gray Wednesday. Even after it was confiscated, it recorded the conversations of the state security agents and the police. They wore no badges and locked us up by force at the Infanta y Manglar station. This recording contains the names of some of those responsible, and it reveals background on police operations against dissidents, independent journalists, and bloggers. I have sent copies of this record of a "kidnapping" to international organizations concerned with human rights, the protection of reporters, and those who defend against institutional abuse. Several attorneys from the Law Association of Cuba have advised me in this.

Although there is little chance that anyone will be brought to account, at least those responsible know their deeds are no longer hidden by silenced victims. Technology allows all of this to come to light.

Media execution

I braid my hair. Nothing is being celebrated today, better I should leave it tangled and dull, but I divide it into three strands that intertwine following a certain logic. The liturgy of combing calms my anxiety, and in the end my hair is orderly while the world remains unruly. I've lived through a weekend of vertigo, and I thought that the ritual untangling of knots would manage to calm my nerves, but it didn't work.

On Friday, May 21, they pronounced my name on the boring *Roundtable* program, linking it to concepts such as "cyber-terrorism," "cyber-commandos" and "media war." A negative mention on the most important official television program is, for any Cuban, social death. It is a public stoning of insults directed at someone who has critical ideas, but has no right to reply. My friends call, alarmed, afraid that my house is already full of the men who dig under mattresses and look behind pictures. I answer the phone, however, in my most jovial tone, "Tell me who denigrates you and I'll tell you who you are," I say. "If you are insulted by the mediocre, the opportunists, slandered by employees of the powerful but dying machinery, take it as a compliment..." and I mutter this like a mantra all night long.

The next day my neighbors, running after the ever-elusive rice, haven't had time nor inclination to watch such boring TV. What is happening here, where the "media executions" don't work any more? A few years ago, the government bullets of contempt would have kept everyone away. Now they sidle up to me, give me a wink and a thumbs-up. Defamation has been used as a weapon for so long that the incendiary adjectives have lost their power over a people sick and tired of so many slogans and so few results.

Healing balm arrived the same Saturday. An Argentinian snuck my Premio Perfil Award into the country, and almost simultaneously a Chilean managed to get the Spanish edition of book through customs, wrapped in pink paper.

Fish eyes

They are there to watch and record us. Dozens, hundreds of cameras scattered throughout the city, as if it were not enough that there are vans filled with police, the Committees for the Defense of the Revolution (CDRs) on every block, and the security forces in checked shirts. They have been installed with an efficiency rarely seen in the execution of any project for public benefit. Their sophisticated structure is the same on streets where half the houses are on the verge of falling down as in the modern tourist enclaves and on the sumptuous Fifth Avenue. They capture those who traffic in beef, sell drugs, or steal a gold chain; but they also monitor those who don't keep guns under their beds, but rather opinions in their heads.

When these "fish eyes" began to be installed everywhere, they generated a sense of paralysis among Havanans. I remember looking for blind spots where the crystal globes couldn't see me. Then I relaxed a little and learned to live with them, though I still felt the itch on the back of my neck of a person who knows she is being observed. Among the speculations about these filming devices is one that they have face-detection programs—including a database—that read anthropometric measurements. But comments of this kind may well belong to the fantasy catalog generated by everything new.

These public cameras—the embodiment of the Orwellian "telescreen"—have ushered in a new cinematography. Although they basically operate automatically, some hands have leaked their contents to the alternative information networks. Dozens of images are emerging from the police archives and circulating right now, by flash memory. Videos in which we see ourselves committing crimes, surviving, stealing, and rebelling. Minutes of police beatings, car crashes, and images of prostitution between young boys and tourists twice their age. One is a complete and shocking snuff movie, which for weeks jumped from one screen to another, from cell phones to DVD players.

Without intending it, the police have given us the crudest testimony they could about our present reality. A succession of scenes that, no doubt, will be stored in the visual memory of this country.

For rent: a little emotion

The man entered the small El Condor bookshop across from the University of Zurich. "I am looking for books by Corin Tellado," he whispered softly. I detected a Havana accent, perhaps because he had spent so little time in contact with the Swiss-German dialect that would eventually change the cadence of his words. He said he was from the La Vibora neighborhood and that he "desperately" needed some Spanish magazines similar to *Hello*.

Maria Mariotti, the owner, said she didn't have anything on hand, but that she could order something from the distributor. "What titles do you want?" asked the small, half-Peruvian, half-Japanese woman. "Anything you can get. They're for my mother, who lives for them," he said, trying to justify his seeming interest in romance. It turns out that having no money to send, every month he tries to send his family publications to support their business of renting magazines like *Vanities* and *People*. For five Cuban pesos, readers eager for the latest issues can keep the magazines for a week, and then they are passed from hand to hand until they fall apart and have to be taken out of circulation.

A few days after that particular order, Maria went to 2003 Barcelona Bookfair, where she met Maria del Socorro Tellado Lupez. She told her about the family in Havana who survived each month thanks to her pen. The author of *Painful Deception* was touched by the story, and she donated a selection of fifty titles, along with a handwritten letter to the lady in La Vibora. That gift caused a burst of thanks from the son of the alternative librarian. He knew well what these added volumes meant. Their pages would provide one household with more soap, some oil, a bit of bread, and shoes for the children, along with dreams for dozens of neighbors.

The horror from the sweetness

In one of life's random events I came across *Letters from Burma* by Aung San Suu Kyi in a Havana bookstore. I didn't find it in one of the private stalls selling used books, but in a local State store that sells colorful editions in convertible currency. The small volume was mixed with self-help manuals and recipe books. I looked around to see if someone had put the book there just for me, but the employees were sleeping in the midday heat. One of them was brushing flies off her face without paying me any mind. I bought the valuable collection written by this dissident between

1995 and 1996, still surprised to find it in my country, where we, like her, live under a military regime with strong censorship of the written word.

Aung San Suu Kyi's chronicles—reflections on everyday life mixed with political discourse and questions—have barely touched down on my shelves. Everyone wants to read her calm descriptions of a Burma marked by fear, yet steeped in a spirituality that makes her current situation all the more dramatic. In the few months since I found the *Letters*, her vivid and moving prose has influenced how we look at our own national disaster. The thread of hope she weaves into her words instills in them her optimistic prognosis for her nation and for the world. No one has been able to describe the horror as she has, without cries overwhelming her style or rancor being reflected in her eyes.

I can't stop wondering how this Burmese dissident's book made it into my country. Perhaps in a bulk purchase? Someone slipped in the innocent-looking cover—an oriental woman with flowers tucked behind her ear, as beautiful as her face. Maybe they thought it was from some fiction writer or poet, creating landscapes of her country out of nostalgia. Probably whoever put it on the shelf didn't know about her house arrest, or the richly deserved Nobel Peace Prize she won in 1991. I prefer to imagine that someone was aware that her voice had come to us. An anonymous face, hands quickly putting the book on the shelf, so that we could recognize our own pain.

The first sip of water

After 134 days without solid food, or even a sip of liquid, Guillermo Fariñas lifted a red plastic cup to his lips and drank a little water. It was 2:15 in the afternoon on Thursday, July 8. On the other side of the glass in the intensive-care unit, dozens of friends burst into applause as if they had witnessed a miracle.

Fariñas had won one battle but still remains in a fierce war against death. The battleground is his own body—ultimately the only space for him to carry out this campaign. His intestines are now like fragile paper distilling bacteria through their pores, his jugular vein is partially obstructed by a blood clot that, if detached, could lodge in his heart, brain, or lungs. He has suffered four staph infections, and a sharp pain in his groin barely allows him to sleep.

His shriveled esophagus was not ready for that first sip of water. It created such a pain in his chest that for a minute he thought he was having a heart attack. But he endured it in silence. On the other side of the glass, expectantly watching, were those who for days had been keeping a vigil outside the hospital, praying for his life. Others had come from afar to ask him to end his martyrdom and to witness his victory. Not wanting to dampen the celebration of jubilant colleagues, he managed to turn a grimace into a smile.

Guillermo Fariñas's family allowed me to watch over him on this first night, after the end of his hunger strike. He allowed me to witness his suffering, his occasional crankiness, and his human weaknesses. Only then did I discover the true hero of today.

Waiting for orders

An acquaintance of my mother's, who lives very near one of the Ladies in White, told her that they are under orders not to assault the women in white carrying gladioli.[29] The same lady, who until recently sneered in disgust at their masses at Santa Rita and the pilgrimages on Fifth Avenue, today was on the point of shaking hands with Laura Pollán and asking for her autograph.

Perhaps another neighbor, the one who screamed "The worms are rioting!" last March on national television, is now confused and waiting for new orders to resume her cries. Mechanisms of false spontaneity have been exposed by this truce: The manufacture of supposed popular response is only confirmed by this interruption in attacks.

If we follow the logic of official propaganda, the people released from prison in recent weeks had deserved to be preyed upon. Party militants and members of the Committees for the Defense of the Revolution were mobilized for so-called "repudiation rallies," where they spat on, insulted, and knocked about the Ladies in White. Now the energetic troublemakers who defended "the Revolution against the mercenaries in the pay of the imperialists" should be expecting some explanation of the prisoners' release. It would be interesting to see what secret revelations they come up with at Party meetings. If none are forthcoming, will they see themselves as pawns, incited one day and commanded to keep quiet the next?

My mother's acquaintance doesn't hide her confusion. "No one understands. Yesterday, they called us to insult them, and today we're not allowed to touch a hair on their heads," she says. (The truce, brief and fragile, appears to be limited to Havana. In Banes, Orlando Tamayo's mother, Reina, continues to be a victim of the same methods.)

The truth is, here, where it seemed like nothing would ever happen, suddenly anything can happen. At what point did this story begin to change? Perhaps it was in the damp, dark, vermin-filled punishment cell where Orlando Zapata Tamayo sacrificed himself; or in the sterile, chilly intensive care ward where Guillermo Fariñas stuck by his decision to die if the prisoners were not freed; or in the streets of Havana, where some defenseless women defied omnipotent power by screaming the word "freedom" where there was none.

Between two walls

Finally, I sit down in a hotel chair, open my laptop, and glance from side to side. Seeing me, the security guard mutters a brief "she came" into the microphone at his lapel. Afterward some tourists appear. My index finger works the mouse as fast as it can to optimize the few minutes of Internet access. It's the first time in ten days that I've managed to submerge myself in the World Wide Web. A list of proxies helps me with the censored pages. I will see the *Generation Y* portal via an anonymous server, a bridge to banned sites. In three years, I've become a specialist in slow connections, badly performing public cybercafés, and working under surveillance. Blindly, I administer a blog, send tweets I can't read the responses to, and manage a nearly collapsed e-mail account.

In all the barriers to reach cyberspace, censorship grips us from two sides. One side is our government's lack of political will to allow this Island uncensored access to the Web, which shows in the filtered blogs and portals and in the prohibitive prices for an hour of Web access. The other side—also painful—is the services that exclude people in our country because of the anachronistic embargo. Those who think that limiting sites like Jaiku, Google Gears, and App Store will move the authorities of my country are naïve. Those who govern us have satellite dishes, broadband, open Internet, iPhones full of applications, while we—the citizens—trip over screens that say "This service is not available in your country."

Just as we get around the internal restrictions here, we also sneak through the closed gates of exclusions abroad. For every lock there is a trick to picking it open. Still, it frustrates me that after avoiding the State Security agents watching my apartment, paying a third of a monthly salary for an hour of Internet time, and seeing the animosity in the faces of the guards at hotels, I see that Revolico, Cuba Encuentro, Cuba Net and DesdeCuba continue to be censored sites.

I enter a URL, and—instead of opening—it seems like a wall is raised on the other side.

Fidel Castro, present and past

Fidel Castro's return to public life after a four-year absence provokes conflicting emotions here. His reappearance surprised a people waiting, with growing despair, for reforms

announced by his brother Raúl. While some weave fanta-
sies around his return, others are anxious about what will
happen next.

The return of a famous figure is as familiar a theme in
life as it is in fiction—think Don Quixote, Casanova, or
Juan Domingo Perón. But another familiar theme is disap-
pointment—of those who find that the person who returns
is no longer the person who left, or at least not as we remember him. There is often a sense of despair surrounding
those who insist on coming back. Fidel Castro is no excep-
tion to this flaw inherent in remakes.

The man who appeared on the anniversary of "Revolution Day" last week bore no resemblance to the sturdy soldier who handed over his office to his brother in July 2006.
The stuttering old man with quivering hands was a shadow
of the Greek-profiled military leader who, while a million
voices chanted his name in the plaza, pardoned lives, announced executions, proclaimed laws upon which no one
had been consulted, and declared the right of revolutionaries to make revolution. Although he has once again donned
his olive-green military shirt, little is left of the man who
used to dominate television programming for endless
hours, keeping people in suspense from the other side of
the screen.

The great orator of times long past now meets with an
audience of young people in a tiny theater and reads them a
summary of his latest reflections, already published in the
press. Instead of arousing a fear that makes even the brav-
est tremble, he calls forth, at best, a tender compassion. After a young reporter calmly asks a question, she follows up

with her greatest wish: "May I give you a kiss?" Where is the abyss that for so many years not even the most courageous dared to jump?

A significant sign that Fidel Castro's return to the microphones has not being going over well is that even his brother refused to echo, in his most recent speech to parliament, the former leader's gloomy prognostication of a nuclear Armageddon that will start when the United States launches a military attack against North Korea or Iran. Many analysts have pointed out that the man who was known as the Maximum Leader is hardly qualified to assess the innumerable problems in his own country, yet he turns his gaze to the mote in another's eye. This pattern is familiar, with his discussions of the world's environmental problems, the exhaustion of capitalism as a system and, most recently, predictions of nuclear war. Others see a veiled discontent in his apparent indifference toward events in Cuba. Yet this thinking forgets the maxim: Even if he doesn't censure, if Caesar does not applaud, things go badly. It is unthinkable that Fidel Castro is unaware of the appetite for change that is devouring the Cuban political class; it would be naïve to believe that he approves.

For years, so many lives and livelihoods have hung on the gestures of his hands, the way he raises his eyebrows or the twitch of his ears. Fidel watchers now see him as unpredictable, and many fear that the worst may happen if it occurs to him to rail against the reformers in front of the television cameras.

Perhaps this is why the impatient breed of new wolves does not want to stoke the anger of the old commander, who is about to turn eighty-four. Some who intended to introduce more radical changes are now crouching in their spheres of power, waiting for his next relapse.

Meanwhile, those who are worried about the survival of "the process" are alarmed by the danger that his obvious decline poses to the myth of the Cuban revolution personified, for fifty years, in this one man. Why doesn't he stay quietly at home and let us work, some think, though they dare not even whisper it.

We had already started to remember him as something from the past, which was a noble way to forget him. Many were disposed to forgive his mistakes and failures. They had put him on some gray pedestal of the history of the twentieth century, capturing his face at its best moment, along with the illustrious dead. But his sudden reappearance upended those efforts. He has come forward again to shamelessly display his infirmities and announce the end of the world, as if to convince us that life after him would be lacking in purpose.

In recent weeks, he who was once called The One, the Horse, or simply He, has been presented to us stripped of his captivating charisma. Although he is once again in the news, it has been confirmed: Fidel Castro, fortunately, will never return.

Inside the neighborhood, outside the heart

"You must turn in your passport!" So they told him on his arrival in Caracas, to prevent him from making it to the border and deserting. In the same airport they read him the rules: "You cannot say that you are Cuban, you cannot walk down the street in your medical clothes, and it's best to avoid interacting with Venezuelans." Days later, he understood that his mission was a political one, because more than curing heart problems or lung infections, he was supposed to examine consciences and probe voting intentions.

In Venezuela he saw the corruption of some of those in charge of the Barrio Adentro Project. The "shrewd ones" here become the "scoundrels" there. They grabbed power, influence, and money, even pressuring single female doctors and nurses to become their concubines. They placed him, with six other colleagues, in a cramped room and warned them that if they were to die—victims of all the violence out there—they would be listed as deserters. But it didn't depress him. He was only twenty-eight, and this was his first time away from his parents, the extreme apathy of his neighborhood, and the shortages in the hospital where he worked.

A month after he arrived, they gave him an identity card and told him he could vote in upcoming elections. At a quick meeting it was explained what a hard blow it would be to Cuba to lose such an important ally in Latin America. "You are soldiers of the Fatherland," they shouted at them, and as such, "you must guarantee that the red tide prevails at the polls."

Now the days when he thought he would save lives or relieve suffering are long gone. He just wants to go home, return to the protection of his family, and tell his friends the truth, but for now he can't. First he must stand in line at the polls, show his support for the Venezuelan Socialist

Party, hit the screen with his thumb as a sign of agreement. He counts the days until the last Sunday in September. After that, he believes, he can go home.

Celebration

I so regret not having an Internet connection on days like this, to share so much happiness with the blog's commentators. Clacking keyboards, drinking toasts screen to screen, and thanking all of you who have supported me with your encouragement, your critiques, and your suggestions.

Three years ago, the shy woman I once was opened this virtual space to narrate her reality, with more fears than certainties. I remember the incredulity of the first readers, the doubts of some, the State Security or CIA card others assigned me, the slip-ups on the arduous journey of opinion. From 2007 until now, I feel I have lived six or seven lives, full of achievements but also marked by constant pressure from a repressive apparatus.

As I am a chronic optimist, however, I'm only going to focus on the satisfactions: the growing alternative blogosphere, cracks that have opened in the wall, the podcast inaugurated a few weeks ago, and all the text messages I've received congratulating me on the International Press Institute's World Press Freedom Hero Award, and today, September 6, the great surprise of the 2010 Prince Claus Award.

Broken promise

I swore never again to speak of that gentleman with the

well-trimmed beard and the olive-green uniform who dom-
inated every day of my childhood with his constant presence. I support my decision not to refer to Fidel Castro with
more than one argument: He represents the past; we need
to look forward, to a Cuba where he no longer exists; and
in the midst of the challenges of the present, to allude to
him seems an unpardonable distraction. But today he once
again crashed into my life with one of his characteristic out-
bursts. I feel obliged to focus on him after he declared to
journalist Jeffrey Goldberg that "the Cuban model doesn't
even work for us anymore."

If I recall correctly, they expelled Communist Party
members for less, purged innumerable Cubans, sentencing
them to long terms in prison. The Maximum Leader systematically pointed out those who tried to explain that the
country wasn't working, and they were punished. And we
were all forced to wear the mask of subterfuge in order to
survive on this Island he tried to remake in his own image. Pretense, whispers, deceit, all to hide the very same
opinion that the "resuscitated" Commander now flippantly
tossed out to a foreign journalist.

Perhaps it was a fit of honesty, as comes over the elderly when they assess their lives. It could even be another
desperate play for attention, like his prediction of an im-
minent nuclear debacle or his late *mea culpa* for repressing
homosexuals that he issued with a few weeks ago. To see
him acknowledge the failure of "his" political model makes
me feel like I'm watching a scene where an actor gesticu-
lates and raises his voice so that the public won't look away.
But as long as Fidel Castro doesn't take the microphone and

announce to us that his obsolete creature will be dismantled, nothing has actually happened. If he doesn't repeat
the phrase here to us in Cuba, and, in addition, agree not
to interfere in the necessary changes, we're back to square
one.

On hearing the news, a dissident friend called me. His
words were ironic, but true: "If he has joined the opposition,
I'm moving over to the official side."

Olivia

My friend Miguel left, tired of waiting for a sex-change
operation and knowing full well that he would never get
a better job. He left the red wig to a friend who worked in
the same hospital and sold, illegally, the room he had in
Luyanó. The day he asked permission to leave, he put on a
suit and tie, which made him roar with laughter when he
looked in the mirror. At the immigration office, he tried to
keep his hands off his trouser crease, so that a last gasp of
homophobia wouldn't spoil his departure.

He escaped before they closed the river of Cubans that
briefly flowed to Ecuador. His was one of seven-hundred
contracted marriages whose sole objective was residency
in that South American nation. Miguel paid the equivalent
of $6,000 and in return got a wedding in Havana with a
woman from Quito he'd known for a couple of hours. He
faked pictures of the honeymoon, paid off an official at the
Ministry of Public Health to give him his "release," and
even handed over a little cash so his white card—the exit
permit—wouldn't be too terribly delayed. He pretended to

be what he was not, which was easy for him, because those of us born on this Island are good at dissembling.

Now he expects difficult times because the Ecuadorian police have started investigating the 37,000 Cubans who entered that country in recent years. He doesn't seem scared, though. He is gay, one of those they loaded into police trucks under heavy blows. And for years he was monitored for his critical views. After experiencing both edges of censorship's blade, nothing frightens him. When called to testify—if he is called—he will go wearing the red dress he always wanted to wear here. Nobody is going to stop him from gesturing while they interrogate him, because Miguel has already escaped the Miguel he once was, to become—happily—Olivia.

Krazy glue

People are shouting from balcony to balcony. At first I think they're insulting each other, but that's not it. The woman from the building on the corner tells another woman that they have Krazy Glue at the little shop at Boyeros and Tulipán. Both are wide-eyed, gesticulating, "I thought it was gone forever," "There's been none anywhere," they say. I chuckle while looking at the tip of my shoe, greatly in need of this fixative that the neighbors are announcing as if the ration stores had gotten a delivery of beef. If I get there in time to get a tube of the magic, I could fix the computer key that's been flying off, too, and also the doorbell, which you can barely hear when someone rings.

Surrounded by my collection of broken things, I start to

wonder how much Krazy glue is used on the Island each year. It is not a basic product, but I sense a relationship between the need to repair and the seriousness of the country's economic crisis. If not, why is the whole world running to get an adhesive advertised as able to reassemble anything? I often have bits of glue stuck to my elbows or my clothes after making one of the repairs I'm faced with every day. The last time, I ended up with my thumb and index finger glued together, until hot water managed to separate them, taking off a piece of skin in the process.

In many stores, when this contact cement comes in you'd think there was a huge sale. People buy dozens of tubes, as if its great adhering power could glue together a reality cracked by frustration. We are not an excessively austere people who can't stand to throw out useless things, but we find it difficult to pay attention to expiration dates provided by manufacturers. When we break something, we rarely have a substitute. So I will leave this post here, and go and buy my share of Krazy Glue, my necessary dose of that instantaneous mender. Perhaps a few drops will help me mend the pieces of that future we've dropped on the floor and smashed to smithereens.

Tropical Sakharov

It's difficult to imagine that inside the frail body of Guillermo Fariñas, behind the face with no eyebrows, is a willingness to confront discouragement. It is also surprising that even when his health was most critical, he never stopped caring about the problems and difficulties of those around him. Even now, with his gallbladder removed and painful stitches crisscrossing his abdomen, whenever I call him he always asks after my family, my health, and my son's school. This man has such a way of living for others! It's no wonder that he refused food so that fifty-two political prisoners would be released.

There are prizes that impart prestige to a person, that shine a light on the value of someone who, until recently, was unknown. But there are also names that add luster to an award, and that is the case with the Sakharov Prize for Freedom of Thought awarded to Fariñas. After this October, future recipients of this highest laurel of the European Parliament will have one more reason to be proud. Because now the prize has an even greater value for being awarded to this man from Villa Clara, an ex-soldier who renounced arms to throw himself into the peaceful struggle.

Who better for this award than he, who undertook an immense challenge and accomplished it, who has given us all a lesson in integrity, who has subjected his body to pains and privations that will affect the rest of his life? There is no name more fitting to join a list that includes Nelson Mandela, Aung San Suu Kyi, and Cuba's Ladies in White. A straightforward man, this journalist and psychologist, whom neither the microphones, nor all the journalists who have interviewed him, nor all the recent cameras' flashes have managed to change. With a modesty so admired by his friends, Coco—because even his nickname is humble—has made the Sakharov Prize seem that much more important.

The mandarins come by boat

The mesh bag has five mandarin oranges inside. They've come from Europe with a reader who discovered where I live thanks to tracks in the blog. He took the citrus fruits out of his backpack—a little embarrassed—as if giving me something too common on this Island, even more common than the invasive marabou weed, or than intolerance. So why do I grab the bag and bury my nose in every fruit? I shout for my family while sinking my nails into the orange globes and smelling my fingers, a celebration of orange zest on each hand.

A trail of peels covers the table and even the dog gets excited about the scent wafting through the whole house. Mandarins have arrived! My niece is thrilled and I have to explain that once these fruits did not come to this Island by boat or plane. To avoid confusing her—she's only eight—I omit the history of the National Citrus Plan, the large Isle of Youth groves where oranges and grapefruits were harvested by students from other countries. Nor do I mention false State statistics, or Tropical Island brand juices, initially made from pulp extracted from our own crops but now made from imported syrup. But I do tell her that when November and December rolled around, all the children in my elementary school smelled like oranges.

What days those were! When no one had to bring us, from a far-off continent, what our own land could produce.

Cultural dysgraphia

Claudia Cadelo is still waiting to hear from the Provincial

Prosecutor about her complaint over the cultural apartheid at a recent Young Filmmakers Exhibition. Agent Rodney never showed his face to confirm or deny the sad events of November 2009. And plainclothes police, under no order from any court, surround the home of Luis Felipe Rojas. My formal complaint for the beating and false arrest I suffered in February has met only silence from the legal institutions, while Dagoberto Valdés still waits for an explanation of why he can't travel outside Cuba. We are surrounded by a repression that does not sign papers, show its face, or place a stamp next to each act that violates its own laws.

Punishments that leave no evidence, detainees who do not appear on the inmate log of any police station, threats from voices that leave no trace. A culture of intimidation without a written language, imposed by pseudonymous agents who coerce but leave no marks. When we demand that they put in writing the phrases they scream at us—in rooms far from cameras and microphones—they tighten their lips and boast about anonymous power. If we formally appeal to laws they themselves created, thirty, sixty, ninety days pass, and nothing. No judge will hear a complaint against the olive-green institution that rules this country.

So vainglorious from the dais, they use words like "courage," "sacrifice," and "fortitude" as they hide behind their own fear and avoid putting their names, their faces, and their convictions next to the atrocities they commit.

My dangerous book

In March of this year, ten copies of the Spanish edition of

my book entitled *Cuba Libre* were shipped to me via DHL, which turned them over to the government, which confiscated them. I filed a complaint to retrieve my property and now, November 25, all these months later, have finally received an answer. With five statements of "Fact," the Inspector of Customs Control justifies the seizure. "Fact No. 3" is the heart of the matter:

> *"The contents of the book* Cuba Libre *are against the general interests of the nation, since it argues that certain political and economic changes are required in Cuba so that its citizens may have more material benefits and achieve personal fulfillment, ends completely contrary to the principles of our society."*

NOTES

1. The Special Period: In a January 1990 speech, two months after the fall of the Berlin wall, Fidel Castro warned of coming hardships and first used the phrase "a special period in a time of peace." When the Soviet Union collapsed in 1991, its 30 years of subsidies to Cuba came to an abrupt end. Oil imports dropped 90%, industry was paralyzed, agriculture shifted from machines to manual labor, food rations shrank precipitously and hunger became widespread. Yoani was 14 when the "Special Period" began.

2. "The boys of the apparatus" whom Yoani also often refers to as "the restless boys," are state security employees and agents (of any age). They include the "physical" enforcers of the state, as well as those who sit in front of computers harassing and threatening bloggers and trying to bring down their websites. The "restless boys" have successfully blocked Yoani's website in Cuba, where it cannot be accessed from public portals.

3. Fidel Castro formed the first microbrigades in 1970 to address the country's housing crisis. Each workplace chose a group of people who were paid their regular salaries to work with professional builders to construct apartments. On completion, the units were assigned to the "most deserving," not necessarily the microbriga-distas themselves. Yoani's husband, Reinaldo Escobar, was a part of the microbrigade that built the building where they now live.

4. The Black Spring refers to March 18–21, 2003, when, with the world's attention focused on the American invasion in Iraq, the Cuban government arrested seventy-five journalists, librarians, and democracy and human rights activists. Charged with working as agents of the United States, they were sentenced to terms ranging from six to twenty-eight years. Some were released at the time,

but as of this post, most remained in prison. In 2010 the Catholic Church brokered a deal with the government to release all the Black Spring prisoners, but at the end of the year those who refused to go into exile remain behind bars.

5. Cuba has two currencies: Cuban pesos, also known as "national money," and Cuban convertible pesos, or CUCs. Workers' wages are paid in Cuban pesos, worth roughly four cents in US currency. Foreign visitors to the island must convert their money to Cuban convertible pesos (CUCs), worth roughly one US dollar. Goods and services in Cuba are sold in both currencies, but many everyday items are available only in CUCs. Prices for items sold in CUCs are roughly comparable to prices in the US or higher. The average monthly wage in Cuba is roughly four hundred fifty Cuban pesos, or the equivalent of eighteen US dollars.

6. Peso stores sell their merchandise only in Cuban pesos. See note 5, above.

7. Fidel Castro coined the term "Battle of Ideas" during the custody battle over Elian Gonzalez, the 6-year-old lone survivor of a group of Cuban rafters, rescued from an inner tube off the coast of Florida in 2000. When Fidel passed the presidency to his brother Raúl in 2008, he stated, "My only wish is to fight as a soldier in the Battle of Ideas."

8. The Malecón is the name of the seawall along the Havana waterfront, a major gathering place for Habaneros.

9. The Piragua is an open space along the Malecon near the Hotel Nacional, where concerts and other celebrations are often staged. During Carnival, the date of which moves around the calendar according to the government's whim, the Piragua is filled with kiosks selling food and drink.

10. The Maleconazo was a spontaneous anti-government

demonstration that flared along the Malecon on August 5, 1994, apparently sparked by news that the ferries crossing Havana Bay were being hijacked and leaving for the United States. Fidel Castro went to the Malecon to calm the disturbance, accompanied by paramilitaries armed with iron bars, but when he left the demonstration reignited. Six days later, Fidel Castro announced that the government would no longer prevent Cubans from leaving by sea. This resulted in the Rafter Crisis, in which over 30,000 people left by sea for the United States in one month.

11. *Jinetero* (male) and *jinetera* (female) literally means "jockey" and is a slang term for prostitute.

12. *Cubiche* is derogatory slang for a Cuban.

13. El Cobre, a copper mining town near Santiago de Cuba, is the site of the Sanctuary of Cobre dedicated to Cuba's patron saint, the Virgin of Charity, nicknamed "Cachita." The church houses a small statue of the Virgin Mary which was found floating in the sea off the Cuban coast in the early 1600s. Visitors to Cachita's shrine leave gifts, which range from Olympic medals to everyday objects. These gifts are not censored or removed by the State. Visitors also take away with them copper stones from the mines.

14. Yoani and her husband Reinaldo began the Blogger Journey, and then the Blogger Academy, to educate people on how to use the Internet and to grow the alternative blogosphere on the Island.

15. *Voces Cubanas* (Cuban Voices) is a newly-created website hosting the blogs of alternative Cuban bloggers. It can be found at: www.vocescubanas.com.

16. "Take Me Sailing on the Wide Sea" is the name of a popular Cuban children's song.

17. Miguel Barnet is the national president of Union of Writers and Artists of Cuba (UNEAC). Yoani is referring to his assertion that

there is complete freedom of travel in Cuba, except for criminals, for which he cited as proof that he himself had traveled to 30 countries. As of the end of 2010, Yoani has been denied a travel permit nine times.

18. *La Jiribilla* is a government-sponsored, web-based cultural magazine. Yoani is frequently attacked in its digital pages.

19. *Almendrones*—derived from the word "almond"—are pre-Revolutionary American cars used as shared taxis.

20. General Arnaldo Ochoa, who fought with Fidel Castro in the Revolution, was the commander of the Cuban troops in Angola, and ultimately, as head of Cuba's Western Army, became the third most powerful person in the country. In 1989 he and several others were arrested and charged with treason in a complex case involving accusations of drug trafficking. He was found guilty and executed by firing squad.

21. CUBALSE was a state-run company formed in 1962 to serve the needs of foreigners in Cuba; it eventually grew to multi-million dollar company operating a wide range of enterprises.

22. Rapid Response Brigades are supposedly groups of workplace or neighborhood "volunteers" who are "ready to defend the Revolution" in their own neighborhoods, with shouts, fists and crude weapons. They are actually well-organized groups, often bused in, who attack any public manifestation of discontent. Photos taken by the bloggers and others have been documenting that the same faces appear in "rapid response" actions at widely dispersed places.

23. A "repudiation meeting" or "act of repudiation" is a public action against any individual or group manifesting discontent. Known dissidents may have their houses surrounded by shouting mobs, may be beaten in the street, or attacked in other ways. Often the targets of these attacks will be detained "for their own protection"

by security agents who "rescue" them "from the mob."

24. July 26, 1953, the date of a failed attack by Fidel Castro and his followers on the Moncada Army Barracks in Santiago de Cuba, is recognized as the beginning of the Cuban Revolution. At the 2007 commemoration ceremony, Raúl Castro devoted about a third of his speech to the problems of milk production. Those who watched the speech live heard him say that these problems would be solved so that every "Cuban can enjoy a glass of milk with breakfast," a line that was later cut from the rebroadcast and printed versions of the speech.

25. Bayamo is a city in eastern Cuba. The Cuban national anthem is a song that was sung during the Battle of Bayamo in 1868, an early effort to gain independence from Spain.

26. F1 cows are a cross of Holstein and Zebu (Cebu) cattle. Fidel Castro believed these cattle would allow Cuba to export beef and dairy products. It didn't work out; both meat and milk are severely rationed in Cuba.

27. In 1970 Fidel Castro turned the resources of the entire country to achieving a record ten-million ton sugar harvest, even "rescheduling" Christmas for July so as not to interfere with the work. The target was missed and Cuba's sugar crop has declined ever since; in 2010 Cuba had its lowest sugar harvest in 100 years, barely over one million tons.

Historically, Cuba exported coffee from plantations in the eastern highlands. With large drops in production after the nationalization of the coffee plantations, Fidel Castro had a plan to grow coffee, using volunteer labor, in a cordon around Havana, despite expert advice that the climate was unfavorable; it didn't work out. Cuba currently imports coffee and Raúl Castro recently announced that it would be mixed with peas to make it go farther.

28. El Corralito was the name given to the Argentine government's freezing of bank accounts, and more specifically US dollar deposits, between December 2001 and December 2002, when that nation was in a financial crisis. The word comes from the Spanish word "corral" which has the same meaning in English.

29. The Ladies in White is a group of wives, mothers, sisters and daughters of political prisoners. The group formed in 2003, two weeks after the arrests of the Black Spring. For seven years the Ladies have attended Sunday mass and then marched in procession to a nearby park, wearing white and carrying gladioli. They have frequently been the victims of acts of repudiation and rapid response brigades.